A Dog Named
BOO

Center Point
Large Print

**This Large Print Book carries the
Seal of Approval of N.A.V.H.**

A Dog Named
BOO

*How One Dog and One
Woman Rescued Each Other—
and the Lives They Transformed
Along the Way*

LISA J. EDWARDS

CENTER POINT LARGE PRINT
THORNDIKE, MAINE

This Center Point Large Print edition
is published in the year 2012 by arrangement with
Harlequin Books S.A.

The names and identifying details of some
characters in this book have been changed.

The text of this Large Print edition is unabridged.
In other aspects, this book may vary
from the original edition.
Printed in the United States of America
on permanent paper.
Set in 16-point Times New Roman type.

ISBN: 978-1-61173-552-9

Library of Congress Cataloging-in-Publication Data

Edwards, Lisa J.
 A dog named Boo : how one dog and one woman rescued each other—
and the lives they transformed along the way / Lisa J. Edwards. —
Center Point large print ed.
 p. cm.
 ISBN 978-1-61173-552-9 (library binding : alk. paper)
 1. Dogs—Anecdotes. 2. Women dog owners—Anecdotes.
 3. Human-animal relationships—Anecdotes. I. Title.
SF426.2.E39 2012b
636.7—dc23
                                                        2012018476

In the end, Boo and the book about Boo has to be dedicated to anyone—man, woman, child, dog, etc.—who has ever felt alone, abandoned or outcast. There is a place for all of us; we just have to keep looking for it.

CONTENTS

A Dog Named
BOO

1
Puppy Love

It isn't just the chocolate and the feel of mischief in the air that I've always loved about Halloween. All Hallows' Eve has always brought a welcome crispness to the air that tempers the oppressive heat and humidity lingering from overlong summers, and it always gives me a sense of beginning as the wheel of the year turns each fall. Halloween 2000 seemed no different from any other. That morning, I had no sense of what awaited me, hidden between a pizza parlor, a liquor store and a dilapidated supermarket that always smelled of bleach and mold. I had no sense of how my life—and hundreds of others'— was about to change.

Driving home from the vet's, I groaned when I realized I needed candy. I couldn't turn around and go to the nicer grocery store; the cats were eager to get home.

I hadn't had any trick-or-treaters last Halloween, but at the time I'd thought it was because we'd just moved to Carmel from New York City. Just sixty miles north of the city, Carmel was a place lost in time and space. If I listened carefully to a gentle breeze, I could almost hear banjos playing the theme song from *Deliverance*. Now that I'd

11

lived here for a while, I knew it was unlikely that hordes of children would be making their way up the dark, scary, quarter-mile driveway to my isolated house in the middle of the woods. I almost went straight home, but a beautiful Friday Halloween like this always brought out more kids than usual, and if one or two failed to calculate the negative cost–benefit of coming up to our house, I wanted to be prepared.

Pressed for time, I pulled into the parking lot of the nearest mall, strode determinedly toward the stinky grocery store, and was stopped in my tracks by the sign.

PUPPIES $49.99.

My legs changed course. My head and my walking stick were both powerless to stop them as they took me toward the green awning of the pet supplies store that had definitely not been there the last time I'd braved Bleach-and-Mold Mart. *No,* I thought to my legs, *not puppies—Kit Kats!* My legs ignored me. My heart reminded me that the last time I'd walked into a store with a "Puppies $49.99" sign, it brought me my first dog, Atticus, and changed my life. My head reminded me that the two dogs and two cats I already had were quite enough. I just needed candy.

"HI THERE!" shouted the young clerk with long brown hair and a pierced lip, a bit too enthusiastically.

"I, ah . . . the sign says you have puppies?" I ventured.

"Poor babies," she said, leading me to the center of the store, where a makeshift cardboard pen surrounded by mountains of pet food held a litter of puppies who couldn't have been more than five or six weeks old. "They were on the doorstep this morning with a note saying they'd just started eating food. I guess somebody figured we'd find them good homes."

There were five of them, three black and two yellow. There was definitely some Labrador in the mix, but the other breeds were anybody's guess. Regardless, the puppies in front of me were adorable. Four of them were bouncing all over and chasing one another around the make-shift corral with typical puppy enthusiasm.

But it was the fifth, the smallest, who drew me in immediately. A smaller baby boy with a black velvet coat and bewildered brown eyes, he was clearly much slower than his littermates and even other puppies his age that I had worked with in puppy classes. He wandered through his siblings' roughhousing, a toddler in a roller derby. They kept knocking him over as they zoomed by, and as soon as he got up, they'd body-slam him to the ground again. When he did manage to get out of their way, he drifted aimlessly around the pen. Like the eight ball in a game of puppy pool set into motion by an invisible cue ball, he bounced uncontrollably off the sides of the box, bumping into one side and veering off, before hitting the other and bouncing off again.

He was in my hand before I knew I had reached out to pick him up.

The tufted fur on his pure-white chest reminded me of a tuxedo bib and matched the snowy spats on his two back paws. His ears were tiny, folded triangles with points that didn't quite touch his jet-black head. He wore a funny, almost distant expression, as if he were listening intently to a faraway sound only he could hear.

Usually puppies squiggle wildly when removed from play by a stranger, but this one didn't squirm at all. Instead, he lay quietly, unmoving, calm and happy to snuggle up against me as I stroked his velvety fur. I raised him just off the ground for thirty seconds to note his constitution—was he confident? comfortable being handled? disoriented?—and as suspected, he just hung there, inexplicably relaxed or confused; it was hard to tell which. I got the sense he didn't even know he wasn't on the floor.

How could I not fall in love with this sweet, helpless little guy who was gazing at me with unquestioning puppy eyes?

The fact that there could hardly be a worse time to bring a new dog into my life was probably exactly the reason the universe put him right in front of me. There were plenty of reasons to put the puppy down and walk away. There was my husband, Lawrence, who was still recovering from emergency surgery. He had gone into the hospital with what we thought was a burst appendix but turned out to be severe, undiagnosed Crohn's disease. The doctors had to remove nearly two feet of small intestines, and he came down with a near-fatal systemwide infection following the surgery. Thankfully, Lawrence was stubborn enough to hang on (part of me thinks he did so just to prove his pessimistic doctors wrong). After months of recovery, he was finally able to go back to his IT management position at a dot-com in White Plains, but he was overwhelmed by the amount of work he had to catch up on, exhausted and in pain most of the time as he struggled to come to terms with all the changes that came with a potentially life-threatening disease. The stress and trauma of it all made my usually fun-loving husband annoyed and irritable, but I was holding onto faith that I'd have my old husband back soon.

After a summer of all of this, a bouncy, playful, energetic puppy was not something either of us envisioned in our lives, not to mention that I had no time for taking care of a new dog. In addition to teaching dog-training classes part time, I commuted several days a week to my office job in New York City, where I managed a couple of literary agencies and tried in vain to sell a manuscript or two. Not only was it a morally defeating job, but it also meant that for three or four days a week, a new puppy would be on his own, confined to a crate, with no one to take care of him or take him out for midday walks (a dog walker in Putnam County was unheard of in those days). There was also the fact that we had a pretty full house of pets as it was, between the cats Merlin and Tara, the black-and-white border collie mix Atticus and our shepherd-Doberman Dante.

A new puppy was the last thing we needed right now. Yet, Atticus was ten, and a puppy might bring him some youthful energy; Dante could always use another playmate; and after the summer we'd had, perhaps a puppy was just what we really needed.

I knew I was rationalizing, but something told me this puppy needed to come home with me. On some level, I related to this little baby dog, and I couldn't bear to let him suffer if I had any control over it.

Of course, I'd never been abandoned in a cardboard box in a strip mall between a pizza parlor and a liquor store, but I knew what it felt like to be bullied. I also knew what it felt like to be abandoned, to be abused by the very people I should have been able to trust the most.

The more I watched him stumble around in the

pen, getting knocked down time and time again, the more the floor gripped at my feet. It was as if I couldn't move until I'd figured out a way to help this little tuxedo-wearing furball. He'd already been abandoned once that day, and it felt horribly wrong to abandon him again.

I believe that fate leads us to the animals we need in our lives—and the animals who need us in theirs. I'd had no intention of getting Atticus or Dante, but they'd both turned out to be blessings beyond compare who had each come into my life for a purpose, from circumstances that mirrored those of my childhood, circumstances I wanted to try to fix in the here and now. In Atticus, I saw an animal alone and scared. In Dante, I saw an animal lost, hungry for love and attention. In this little helpless pup, I saw an animal bullied and abandoned, an animal who just didn't fit in with the other pups, and I couldn't leave that vulnerable little puppy to fend for himself. It was all too familiar.

Bringing the other dogs into my life had worked out, so maybe this would, too.

"I am kind of fond of the little guy, here," I quietly said to the clerk.

"Yeah, I like that one, too."

"I have two dogs at home, though," I said, "and I'd like them to meet him before I decide anything. Can I bring them here and introduce them?"

17

She clearly wasn't ready for that question, but with a little cajoling, I was able to talk the clerk into agreeing to a visit. As I tried to leave the store, a sudden wave of *whoops* came over me. I had thought about the dogs and how they might like the little guy, but I was forgetting about that other person in the household: my husband. Lawrence needed to be onboard, too. I had to get him to see that the puppy needed us as much as I thought we needed him. I braced myself, and as soon as I dialed his number, the spell that was holding me in place broke.

"What?" snapped Lawrence. I could hear the stress radiating from his keyboard as he typed.

"Um . . . I'm looking at a puppy, and . . ."

"Yeah?" *Type type type.*

"And I think you need to come see him."

Type type type. "Why?" *Type type type.*

"Because I think he needs to come home with us."

No typing. "Why?"

"He doesn't fit in—I can't say why. I just can't leave him here." I started to clam up as the words stuck in my chest.

It has always been difficult for me to ask for anything, even from my husband. Years of being bullied, abused and forced to fend on my own had whittled down my confidence, and the end result was a sense of worthlessness that I was trying to sculpt into something healthier but only managed to polish to a brighter sheen. Lawrence's guarded nature, a defense mechanism from his own dysfunctional upbringing, meant he never revealed much of himself. He masked things with a sardonic wit that fit mine like a glove. This became a bit of a hurdle when we were trying to discuss serious topics.

I took a breath and tried again. "He needs us. I just can't walk away. Could you leave work a little early and meet me here? Once you see him, you'll understand."

Lawrence sighed heavily, followed by an even more vigorous *type type type*. Finally: "If I have to."

"He's very sweet," said the clerk after I hung up, "and so soft." I opened my mouth to tell her that he really can be when he's not stressed, but then I realized she was talking about the dog, not my husband. Regardless of his tone of voice, Lawrence is the greatest champion of the underdog I have ever met. I only hoped this little puppy would charm Lawrence the way he'd managed to charm me.

As I loaded Atticus and Dante into the none-too-steady pickup truck for their trip to see the baby dog, they seemed to sense something was up, or maybe they were just reading my excitement. The truck was tricky to navigate on a regular basis and more so when the minuscule amount of space I had in the cab for shifting and steering was filled with big, bulky, excited dogs fogging up the windshield. Eventually arriving back at the pet store, I parked in the shade of the buildings and opened the windows to let in a breeze for the dogs. Waiting for Lawrence, I absentmindedly watched the kids spilling out of the elementary school across the street, dressed as fairy princesses and superheroes. For a moment, the familiar ache set in, and I felt that pang of longing. I always had internal conflicts about parenting. Wanting a family of my own was not enough. I needed to know that I would not be repeating my family's dysfunction and that any child of mine would be loved unconditionally by both parents. After Lawrence's upbringing, he was adamantly opposed to children, also fearing the repetition of old dysfunctional patterns, and I wasn't going to bring a child into a home where only one parent wanted him.

Eventually Lawrence pulled up next to me, looking grumpy. Even four months after his operation, it was still uncomfortable for him to drive for long periods of time, and after what sounded like a particularly stressful day, he couldn't be in too receptive a mood. I left Atticus and Dante in the well-ventilated truck while Lawrence and I went in to see the puppies.

"So, which one is the wonder dog?" he asked. Ignoring the sarcastic tone, I pointed to my tiny new buddy, who was curled up in the corner with his eyes shut, oblivious to his littermates' antics. Lawrence was not impressed. "Is he even alive?"

Momentarily scared because puppies can be so fragile, I gently touched the motionless baby, and as if on cue, little White Chest blinked, let out a tiny yawn and settled back to sleep. "See? He's just tired. Why don't you hold him?"

Lawrence had a flurry of objections: No, he didn't want to hold him; the dog didn't look very healthy, in his opinion; we had enough pets, and he didn't have the time or energy to help raise another one when just going to work was an effort; puppies are a lot of trouble and nuisance; they chewed up shoes; they cried at night; they peed and pooped all over the house.

"Let's see what the boys think," I said, and headed out to the truck.

Atticus, a fiercely loyal, one-woman dog, was as ecstatic to see me as if I'd been gone for days. Once in the store, he was ecstatic to see Lawrence, ecstatic to see the bags of dog food stacked against the walls, and especially ecstatic to sniff the display of rawhide bones. Atticus had never been particularly interested in other dogs, but he glanced at the puppies with a bit of a drive-by sniffing, then became ecstatic about other things in the store. There was no growling, no barking, no snarling, no hard staring. From Atticus, that had to be counted as approval.

I exchanged Atticus for the always ebullient Dante, who was thrilled to see me, thrilled to see Lawrence, thrilled to see the clerk and thrilled to see the puppies, all five of whom—my buddy included—pressed against the side of the pen, paws up as high as they could reach, noses out as far as they could go, trying to get a better look at the dog whose tail was thumping a happy drumbeat on the metal shelving behind him.

"Yes," from Dante.

"Fine with me," from Atticus.

"Okay," said Lawrence, shrugging, "but he's going to be *your* dog, and I'm not driving him home."

We had a consensus . . . of sorts.

I didn't have a crate for White Chest in the truck, and because we had so many leashes at home, I hadn't bought one. As a result, the ride home with our new baby dog was massively treacherous. The roads in our part of Putnam County are usually very curvy, often hilly, sometimes steep and always edged with huge boulders that leave very little room for error. I was continually shifting gears to accommodate the roads while simultaneously trying to hold onto the squirming puppy, who clearly wanted desperately to get out of the big, scary metal box that was making terrifying noises. Pressing him up against me tightly, I briefly let go to shift, then felt around to find him in the dark of the cab. It's a good thing I didn't get pulled over, as I am not sure how I would have explained that it was a puppy and not alcohol causing all the swerving.

Once we got home with the baby dog still in the appropriate number of pieces, Lawrence said, "Remember, this is your dog," before he went to his computer.

I set up one of the cat's crates for the puppy to sleep in, cobbled a playpen together from an old kitchen cabinet without doors, and with close supervision put the little guy on the floor to investigate his new home. After a while, Lawrence came away from his computer to watch the baby dog explore his new world. Arms folded tightly across his chest, Lawrence dispassionately watched the puppy scramble around the kitchen and the dining room, then his face revealed softer and softer lines, and eventually opened into a grin.

Before long, the puppy found Dante lying on his side—a pose that must have reminded the baby of his mother, given the way he started rooting around Dante's belly. Dante picked up his head, eyeing the baby suspiciously, and my face went slowly from a happy look-at-the-nice-interaction face to an uh-oh-what-is-he-doing face to a holy-crap-he's-found-*something*-that-is-clearly-not-a-nipple-and-he's-trying-to-nurse face. With a sudden, indignant growl, Dante's huge snout whisked the confused tyke away, sending him flying across the floor, where he skidded to a halt. Undaunted, the little guy padded back toward Dante, his approach more cautious and respectful this time; little White Chest had no intention of making the same mistake twice. He bounced and bowed in Dante's direction, signaling that he just wanted to play, and Lawrence and I laughed until our sides ached.

This was just why I felt we needed a puppy: laughter had been absent since Lawrence's illness. The little Halloween dog was already starting to work his magic.

Starting that Friday night, we spent the whole weekend brainstorming names for our newest housemate. Halloween began as the Celtic festival of Samhain, when spirits of the dead returned to earth to share wisdom or stir up mischief, so we started there. But we couldn't see saddling a confused little puppy with a name like Samhain or Hallow. Blackie was out of the question, and White Chest was clunky. We looked up Celtic deities, but we couldn't pronounce any of their names. "Here, Hu Gadarn, come on, boy!" and "Good Lleu Llaw Gyffes!" don't exactly roll off the tongue.

We considered other mythological figures, such as Anubis, the Egyptian god of the dead, but our clumsy little furball didn't seem to match that menacing moniker. Sirius, the Dog Star, revered by the ancient Egyptians as the watchdog of the heavens, had a nice ring to it, but the six-week-old pup in front of us was hardly a ferocious guardian of home and hearth.

Maybe we were overthinking this. The bumbling little guy with slightly unfocused eyes wasn't at all like Atticus or Dante, so why were we trying to give him a highfalutin name like theirs? Less intellectual and more of an imp, he needed something simpler. Spirit? Shadow? Ghost? The pattern in his white bib had a spooky face embedded in it, but Lawrence pointed out that this ungainly little pup wasn't exactly gliding underfoot like a spirit. When it came to walls, there were three possible explanations: he thought he really was a spirit and could walk through them, he didn't understand the concept of solid objects or he couldn't see them. All puppies are clumsy, as though their brains and legs aren't in complete cooperation, leaving them tumbling over themselves as their back ends move more quickly than their front; however, this little guy seemed clumsier than most. He didn't tumble and bounce like other puppies; he wandered and bumped into as many chairs, tables and people as he did walls. I thought, All dogs are individuals, and accepted that this puppy was not quite the master of his elements . . . yet.

In spite of his inability to navigate the house and all its contents, he was quite adept in his play with Dante. Although the bigger dog outweighed his little playmate by over eighty pounds, and the puppy's entire body could fit in Dante's mouth, they mouth wrestled and played tug like two old buddies reunited. Dante adjusted his play to match the puppy, and the puppy did his best to keep up with his new best friend.

By the end of that first weekend, White Chest had discovered my ottoman and would peek his baby nose out from inside his little "clubhouse," barking his high-pitched puppy bark as if to taunt, "You can't find me," when of course we could all see the tip of his nose and the white of his chin plain as day. His finest discovery was probably the thrill of chasing Merlin the cat, but when he continued to run headfirst into walls, furniture, the other dogs and me, Lawrence suggested, "How about we call him Klutz?"

On Monday when I told my assistant about the new, nameless pup, she looked at me as if I'd said I spent the weekend trying to figure out how to eat a pickle. "Why don't you just call him Boo?" I practically kissed her. It was short and sweet, with just the right note of mischief— perfect for a playful, confused pup. That evening I held Boo up toward the light and admired his satin belly, the ghost face on his chest and the perfection of each tiny paw. I asked him if he wanted to be called Boo. He remained almost motionless, and then his little tail started to wag, brushing against my arm, soft as a feather. The decision was made.

Like so much else about Boo, his name came unexpectedly and surprisingly. The ultimate surprise about Boo, though, was going to be uncovered much later on, as he worked his magic to heal and warm the hearts of all who met him. Atticus brought me through some of my darkest times, teaching me how to love, how to communicate, how to open up, and ultimately finding me a husband. Dante transformed me from insecure and shy to lively and (somewhat) confident and brought me to dog training, which was quickly becoming my calling.

Dogs had already given me gifts of unconditional love, spirit and recovery. Since the moment Boo nestled against my chest in the pet store, I knew he had his own gifts in store—but just what they were, only time would tell.

2

The Boys and Boo

I'm not one of those people who idealize dogs, as in romanticized characters like Goofy or Lassie, but I am gratefully aware of the symbiotic relationship between dogs and humans. For tens of thousands of years, these two species have managed to maintain a reciprocal bond of fondness. Credit should be given to both for this incredible, long-lasting connection; while humans shared food, warmth and a sense of security, dogs offered the unconditional love and forgiveness so difficult to tease out in many human interactions.

It's hard to say which species brought the bigger piece of pie to the symbiotic banquet, but if I had to decide, I'd award the medal to dogs. Kindness can be difficult for humans. We have to actively teach it to our young, while constructing religious ethics and legal codes to keep us from harming one another. As a group, we struggle to avoid war, and on an individual level, police know that when murder is afoot, the most likely perpetrators are the spouse and family members of the unfortunate deceased. We are meanest to the ones closest to us. We can be an antagonistic species that puts power before love. Our dogs forgive us and often help us find our better humanity.

The majority of *Canis lupus familiaris* live as feral dogs, only peripherally interacting with the nearby humans and never dependent on them for food or affection. Those dogs who *do* live with us return again and again, even to the humans who have choked the air out of them, beaten them, kicked them or shocked them for the purposes of *teaching* them. Why? No research can answer why dogs forgive us—we just know they usually do. An ancient Native American myth suggests a link as old as time:

> The earth trembled and a great rift appeared, separating the first man and woman from the rest of the animal kingdom. As the chasm grew deeper and wider, all other creatures, afraid for their lives, returned to the forest—except for the dog, who after much consideration, leapt the perilous rift to stay with the humans on the other side. His love for humanity was greater than his bond with other creatures, he explained, and he willingly forfeited his place in paradise to prove it.
> —Anasazi dog myth

From my experiences as a trainer and behavioral consultant, I also know that some dogs *don't* forgive; sometimes, even when they do, the forgiveness is partial. A dog may still love his human but refuse a training exercise to avoid the punishment his handler is using. If a dog has been severely mistreated, she may be constantly on guard, never feeling completely safe, and therefore never fully trusting her handler. Dogs aren't perfect; they can fight among themselves and turn on their humans, but it is through their ability to live in the moment, love without reservation and forgive that the universe sends us proof of our better angels.

Confused by his new surroundings, desperate to figure things out and struggling to be wanted by Lawrence, Boo was off to a bit of a rough start. It certainly didn't help that the little guy wasn't taking well to house-training. Yet, Boo had one thing going for him: he could make us laugh. Most dogs respond to laughter from their humans better than they do praise, especially as puppies. I will never know if it was Boo's inherent nature to be a clown, if his bumbling ways of running into things just made him seem so or if he learned that the only positive inter-actions he could get from Lawrence was by eliciting laughter from him. One very cold, snow-covered pee trip outside had my sides splitting so much that Lawrence actually joined us to see what could possibly be so funny.

Only about twelve weeks old, Boo, like most dogs, was fascinated by the first snow of the season—so much so that he couldn't just pee in it, but he needed to investigate it, too. He sniffed gingerly at first until he figured it was safe, and then he inserted his entire nose deep into the snow. He must have taken a deep breath while he was underneath because he suddenly jerked his whole head out of the snow and snorted, blowing a snow cloud out his nose. As funny as that was, it was nothing compared with the snow helmet he was sporting. Just the right consistency to hold together long enough to stick to his face, the snow made him the Abominable Snow-Boo. Snow clung to his whole head and mounded on top of his nose, with enough sticking to his whiskers that they glistened in the twilight. Only his deep-black eyes and his dark, wet nostrils peeked through his white snow mask.

I, of course, started to giggle the moment he blew the snow cloud, but then when the bewildered dark eyes started blinking at me from within the snow helmet, I laughed and laughed so much that Lawrence came out to see what was so funny. Together we watched and laughed as Boo repeated the snow-dunking game for our amusement—looking at us each time his head emerged from the snow as if to ask, "This, right? This is what you like?" After several repetitions of this, Boo began shivering and lifting one frozen paw at a time out of the cold snow. It was clear that he needed to go inside despite the fun he was having. Lawrence continued to chuckle as we took Boo in and even said, "He is very cute." It was in these small moments that I hoped the seed of love and affection for Boo would take hold in Lawrence's heart.

Although Boo could take his time winning over Lawrence, he needed to be safe and fully accepted by all the other animals in the house more quickly. In all the excitement, I had remembered to let the dogs meet on neutral ground before bringing the new pup home, but there was still going to be some settling in. Integrating dogs into a multidog household isn't too different from dating: little by little, they spend increasingly more time doing fun things together, sharing their likes, dislikes and personality quirks. Pretty soon they're either in love or completely over each other. Dante, Atticus, Boo and the cats were all going to have to fall in love with one another if Boo was going to live a happy, safe life.

We've just begun to understand how dogs interact with each other, but we know that it involves communication, loyalty, morality, friendship and respect. Left to their own devices, dogs would choose their own buddies; they'd avoid members of their species who bullied them or treated them brutally. Household pets can't always make their own choices, and when their needs are ignored, the results can be disastrous. Even sometimes when animals can make their own choices, those choices can be horribly bad. The most dramatic example of this was with the Druid Peak pack of wolves reintroduced into Yellowstone, where a brutal female breeding wolf bullied other pack members, killed other wolves' puppies and was eventually murdered by her own pack after her years of violent, injurious regime. Yes, this is the extreme, but I have had many clients who live in an armed camp of locked doors and baby gates to keep their dogs safe from one other. I did not want our house to turn into that.

I wasn't worried about Dante, who was about four years old when Boo arrived and immediately took the teaching and motherly role. Atticus worried me a bit because he kept his distance from the baby dog he undoubtedly viewed as a little punk, and occasionally flashed the puppy some pretty big warning signals.

Only three years before Boo's arrival, Dante had put a sparkle back in Atticus's seven-year-old eyes; they played together constantly, took walks together and went to the dog runs together. Now, Dante was the one who sparkled as he took Little Boy Boo under his big, gangly wing. A natural caretaker, Dante loved Boo like a baby of his own from the moment Boo came into the house, in spite of the attempted nursing mishap. Dante cleaned Boo, played with him, taught him to tug with toys and how to mouth wrestle. They chased each other around the yard, and when play was over, Dante snuggled with Boo on the couch or the oversized chair.

Dante had joined our family in 1997. A starving street dog from the Red Hook section of Brooklyn, he was a shepherd-Doberman mix with a very stern, almost scary look, who seemed like the most unusual nanny for Boo—but he made it work.

Six months after Lawrence and I got married, an unusually warm Friday evening in April suggested to us that Atticus would enjoy a romp at the dog park. Since Atticus typically sat next to me on the benches at dog runs, only occasionally going out to sniff a butt or two before returning to his seat next to me, it was much more likely that Lawrence and I were taking the dog-run excuse to cure our own winter cabin fever and spend some time in New York City's fresh, spring air.

As Atticus and I sat and watched the other dogs play, Lawrence circulated around the dog run, playing with other dogs and eventually stopping to chat with a woman at the other end of the park. Before I could ask what was up when he returned (and something was clearly up; it was written all over his face), he said, "I met a great dog."

I said nothing.

"He needs a home."

I looked at him silently.

"The woman who brought him to the park," he said, speeding up and leaving no pause for me to interject, "already has two intact males at home, and they don't get along with him, so he needs a home, and she's desperately trying to find a home for him, maybe just for the weekend, and she says she'll take him back Monday if it doesn't work out, so I thought that maybe we could—"

Lawrence was silenced by the arrival of a whirling cloud of dirt, wood chips, slobber and the lingering smell of dog poop that blurred my field of vision until a huge nose and equally huge tongue attached to a giant collection of canine skin and bones erupted from the cloud, and I was licked from chin to eyebrows.

"That's what he did to me, too," said Lawrence with a grin. "Can we keep him?"

"Absolutely not."

The dog was a wreck. He was emaciated: every rib was visible, and his hips protruded so far that you could cut yourself on them. Even the muscle mass on his head was gone, leaving his eye sockets protruding like strange goggles that made an odd match with his ears, which were halfway folded like the wings of a small jet airplane. This dog appeared badly neglected and would need an incredible amount of care and attention. Furthermore, even just skin and bones, he still probably came in at around seventy pounds, and our one-bedroom apartment was already far too small for the two humans, two cats and one dog who lived there now.

Absolutely not.

An hour later, we watched as the ebullient, withered dog whirled around our living room, ate two bowls of dog food and played King of the Bed wildly with Atticus until they both passed out. We didn't realize it at the time, but that much food for a starving dog with that much activity was medically a bad idea. We could have easily killed him with kindness. Instead of waking the next day to a dead dog, though, we found an astonishingly vast puddle of poop and worms in the middle of the floor, and he spent the whole day tearing through the apartment like a tornado: pooping, running, jumping, pooping, picking up anything and everything he could get his mouth on, and then pooping some more.

Merlin the cat assumed a position on the bed and didn't seem to move from it for three days. Tara, our other cat, difficult to find under the best of circumstances, became absolutely invisible.

Buried inside all the chaos that was Dante was the sweetest, friendliest dog I had ever met. *This can work,* we kept telling ourselves. *We can make this work.* Then, this canine force of nature took the one moment Merlin was off the bed to jump joyously up where the cat had been and pee all over it. We told the woman she had to take him back, then spent the whole night bawling our eyes out.

Realizing that he was ours for good, we named him after the poet Dante Alighieri, whose *Inferno* describes the journey through the nine circles of hell and back. This dog looked like he'd booked the same travel package.

We were incredibly lucky as we naively watched Atticus, never a demonstrative dog, play all night with the loony bag of bones—a match made in heaven. If I'd had the behavioral knowledge then that I do now, I would never have brought an unknown, intact male dog into such a small space, already occupied by so many other animals, without preparation.

Years later, I was hoping that we might luck out similarly with Boo. Although I hedged my bet by bringing Atticus and Dante to meet Boo at the pet store and by managing the new puppy once home, only time would tell if this would all work out. Although their initial reactions were positive, what if the three of them, like the Druid Peak pack, started having discord that built up over the years? I did not want my boys to grow up in a dysfunctional canine family. I knew what walking a tightrope in a dysfunctional family felt like, and I wouldn't wish it on any other creature for the world.

When I look back at early pictures of Boo and Dante, I am reminded of what took me, a lifetime ago, from Illinois to New York University's photography department. Being dyslexic, I see the world through pictures; I struggle every day in a sea of words when images are what truly make sense to me. The pictures of the ten-pound baby Boo playing with his entire head in the mouth of the ninety-pound Dante, whose jaws gently cradled the baby dog as they guided and cared for him, illustrate mutual love, trust and compassion. The pictures of little Boo climbing on Dante's face show the patience and latitude that Dante gave to his little charge, while Boo is completely comfortable with his mammoth brother.

These were not unlike the candid family photos of me as a little kid with my brother, Chuck, and our dog, Princess, showing a happy little girl next to her dog and her bespectacled brother— two super-blond, super-skinny kids with silly expressions hugging a happy dog. I was a cute little waif of a thing with a pixie haircut and a bright pixie smile in those pictures because I knew that when it was just Chuck and me, nothing horrible would happen.

Chuck taught me how to shoot baskets from the free-throw line in the driveway and how to hit a baseball. I spent hours shooting baskets when he was with me and when I was alone. I never learned to love any game, but to this day I still find shooting baskets therapeutic.

During the summer, Chuck and I would ride our bikes to the local pool, where he swam and I stood in the shallow end, afraid to put my head underwater. The point wasn't swimming but spending time with my big brother. We would go on day trips to various places, like Adventure-land and Santa's Village. We would go to the science museum and walk through the giant, oversized heart or explore the old German U-boat. We'd go to Brookfield Zoo and watch, fascinated, as the Mold-A-Rama machine injected gooey plastic into the animal molds so we could bring home dolphins, elephants and polar bears—eagerly scraping the edges clean where the two halves of the mold came together. I think our favorite was going to baseball games at Wrigley Field. Each year, we would sit in a box seat between home plate and third base. It became part of one of the more powerful and profound memories that Chuck and I had.

During the school year, when Chuck wasn't out with his friends or at practice for one of his sports teams, we would share quiet times together watching old movies. Along with Dean Martin and Jerry Lewis movies and every Frank Capra film ever made, science fiction and World War II movies were high on the list. At the very top was

Von Ryan's Express. We always quoted the last line together: "I once told you, Ryan, if only one gets out, it's a victory." We could both recite the entire scripts of *It's a Wonderful Life* and *Miracle on 34th Street*. During the commercial breaks of our movie festivals, Chuck would challenge me to a game of chess and beat me handily before the movie started again. It is a sad thing to admit that I could begin and lose a complete game of chess in the time it took to advertise a few products.

The photos of Boo with Atticus tell a different tale, just as the old pictures of me with my sister, Sue, and my parents show a different little girl: painfully shy, withdrawn, holding her breath, an invisible shadow somehow blotting out the bright pixie seen elsewhere. When I look at these pictures and see my sister—who is almost identical to me but eight years older, without the pixie haircut or the pixie grin—she seems to be always sneering at something unseen. In one picture of Atticus and Boo, Atticus is showing clear and dramatic bared teeth to Boo, who is looking desperately for his big brother's approval. When Atticus would offer punishment like this, Boo would try to shrink away as if trying to make himself invisible so he could go unnoticed. But being Boo, he kept coming back to Atticus, each time trying a different approach to win the older spotted dog's love the same way I would tiptoe time after time into the den to seek out my sister's company, and time after time she'd snap, "Get lost." Because Atticus had all the patience and wisdom of his namesake Atticus Finch from *To Kill a Mockingbird*, Boo was occasionally successful in soliciting play with Atticus, so I was guardedly optimistic that Boo's relationship with Atticus would be better than mine with my sister.

Atticus showed up in my life in 1990—ten years before Boo—when I was single and sharing a Manhattan apartment with friends. One of my roommates, Rob (who was also my boyfriend at the time), was looking for work and had a good deal of time between interviews. I suggested that it might be the perfect time for him to get the dog he wanted because he'd be able to devote all his energy to a new animal while still looking for work. I was a cat person at that time and didn't know exactly what one did with a dog—my memories of Princess had long faded, save for the pictures.

This theoretical dog became a reality one late autumn afternoon when I walked past a pet store on Third Avenue with that fateful sign in the window: "Puppies $49.99." A cowering, black-and-white border collie mix with floppy ears—one speckled, one black—and a matching patch over his left eye, he was as far back in the poop-and-pee-covered cage as he could possibly go.

His body shook as I pulled him out of the cage, and in spite of the fact that he smelled like a filthy combination of puppy breath, poop and pee, I couldn't keep myself from wrapping him in my jacket for warmth and comfort, and of course he never left the inside of my jacket until he was safely home. Once there, I reminded Rob of the strict rules we'd discussed: Atticus wasn't allowed to sleep in our beds, sit on the furniture or be fed from the table.

Every dog is the cutest dog in the world to his own family, and Atticus matured from the cute waif to a handsome dog sporting the classic white body with black spots. His speckled right ear was almost always upright, and his black left ear was almost always flopped over. He was easily identified by the one particularly large, black spot on his rump. In the mid-sixty-pound range, he was a nice size. His lineage was anybody's guess. The store said he was a shepherd-Lab mix, and the veterinarian said he was a terrier mix. None of these accurately described Atticus. His behavior was probably a better indicator of his lineage. In temperament, size and smarts, I could easily have been persuaded that he had cattle dog or border collie in him.

Within a week, the first two dog rules flew out the window. The first time Atticus crawled under the covers with me, I didn't have the heart to push him away. Before long, the fluffy pup was snuggling on the couch with all of us while we watched TV and sleeping regularly on my side of the bed.

It had been years, even decades, since I'd had a dog, but I shouldn't have been surprised by how quickly I returned to my early affinity for them. More than half of the pictures of me as a child are with our dog, Princess, a springer spaniel who joined the family around the same time I did. I clung to her for every ounce of support I could; she gave me the affection that most of my family couldn't or wouldn't. In the family album, there's a series of photos of me as a wobbly toddler dressed in a diaper, robe open and flowing free, feeding Princess the leftover ice cream in my bowl. Another photo from that night shows me proudly sitting on Princess's house-training newspaper, with her sniffing around the area as if wondering what to make of me being in her potty spot. The caption, written in my father's careful, sarcastic hand, reads, "Child Prodigy."

Princess wasn't in our formal family pictures. My mother orchestrated those photos, and they showed a family dressed to deceive. Princess was too open with her emotions and would have given away my mother's photographic subterfuge. My sister and I wore perfect little dresses, and my brother wore a miniature suit and tie to match my father's. My mother was in an elegantly tailored suit, red or aqua, whose measurements were exact, just as she liked everything to be. She was a harsh and unforgiving woman whose rage, usually masked by a social, smiling exterior, was all too easily ignited by anything which threatened to expose the reality beneath her perfect facade. She wore her dark hair styled up; during her weekly visits to the hairdresser, she would settle under the beehive dryers that, along with enough hairspray to single-handedly deplete the ozone layer, offered the promise, both literal and figurative, of a hairdo helmet, protection against whatever the world might throw at her. Whether the pockmarks on her face were from acne or chicken pox, I never had the courage to ask. The formal suits she wore for teaching were made more severe by her refusal to put on any makeup other than lipstick, and though slightly overweight around the middle, she was always a slender woman. Who could think that such a small body could contain such vast stores of rage and such an endless capability for manipulation?

I can only guess at some of the reasons it was so easy for my mother to fly off the handle. In some ways, she herself walked a tightrope of a kind. Her response to her own difficult childhood and troubled marriage was a struggle to pretend that she and everything around her were perfect—and to punish that which was not. All through my childhood, she had to choose between keeping up with my father drink for drink or, during her sober periods, enduring the clever insults he threw at her and the rest of us. She chose the former much more often than the latter, which meant that she would pass out long before the evening was over. I learned early on not to wake her when this happened.

"May I take the curlers out of my hair?" I asked once after rousing her from her stupor the night before Easter. "It's all dry."

"Sure," she slurred, "go ahead." I went to the bathroom to begin the long process. By the time I came out of the bathroom, uncurlered, she was fully awake. When she saw me, her eyes widened, and she rushed over and grabbed my arms in her vise grip. "What. Did. You. Do?" she hissed.

"You said I could take my curlers out, so I—"

"Liar!" she said, her hands tightening even further. "I never said that. I would never let you take your curlers out the night before such an important holiday!" Then she began to shake me, gripping my arms so tightly that she left black-and-blue handprints. My Easter dress had long sleeves, so the next day the bruises didn't show.

As a counterbalance to my merciless, cold mother, my father was a tortured soul who exorcised his inner demons through drink, sarcasm, rage and sex. In one picture, he's leaning over me, smiling, as my mother cuts the cake. But in reality, around the same time, he was demoted from superintendent of schools in Woodstock, Illinois (a job he'd held for only a year) to assistant superintendent of schools in Villa Park. The whispers suggested that this was because of his drinking and a scandal with a woman. Like Mom, he cultivated a proper image for himself that included a good deal of hairspray to make sure that the few strands of hair he had left didn't betray their loneliness (between the two of them, I think, he and my mother kept the hairspray industry in business). His horn-rimmed glasses acted as a constant blood-pressure gauge. If he was looking at you through the glasses, you were okay, but if he was looking over them, you were in deep trouble. To the rest of the world, he was an attractive man who looked a little like Johnny Carson, but to me, he was a terror.

Drunken bad choices led him to many mistakes. Among those was the most inappropriate behavior imaginable—acts that traumatized me for years and years to come. I lived in fear of my father and his nighttime visits for two to three years, from the time I was around six until I was about eight or nine. Survival instincts took over, and my mind tried to block out the horrors I could not control. After a while, it all just blurred together for me, as my brain did what it had to do to get by. I never knew what night would be the night Dad would detour from his path to his room and stop by mine. I would lie in bed facing away from the door, hoping not to hear the footsteps as I anxiously folded the corner of the bedsheet over one way then the other, hoping he would go straight to his bedroom. On the nights he uneventfully passed by my room to his own and I heard my parents' door close, I could finally fall asleep.

On those nights when he stopped by my room, I was told to be quiet as he climbed into bed with me. I closed my eyes and held my breath while a huge hand that smelled of smoke covered my face until he was done. "You can't tell anyone about this," he'd say, "especially not your mother. Do you understand how much it would hurt her feelings? You don't want to hurt your mother's feelings, do you?" On those nights, I would lull myself to sleep by imagining that I could live in my closet—like my own little fort that no one could enter. As instructed, I never said anything to anyone. I didn't really have the words to describe what was going on until years later, when I was able to peel back the layers of self-loathing and feelings of dirty, unloved loneliness.

Who would I have talked to anyway? My sister? She made it clear that she wasn't interested in anything I had to say. My brother? He would have cared, but how would he have protected me from that—and how would I have brought it up to him?

As siblings, we were not encouraged to talk among ourselves. Instead, my parents treated us like Cold War combatants who needed to be separated and handled, lest we band together and rise up against them. It was often more about what wasn't said or shared in our house. Years later, my parents worked very hard to paint over this dysfunction and portray a happy family in the suburbs. I am reminded of this each time I look at the photo albums my father put together in his retirement. Desperate to make the family look cohesive and happy, in several photos he actually cut out pictures of different family members and pasted them together as if we were happily sitting together. If you look closely, you can see the physical division in the picture that so dramatically reflected reality.

Photos of Atticus, Dante and Boo never had to be cut up to contrive a happy family. I set up mutual fun time for them all, like bone time, when they each got a bone to chew and crunch to their delight as they hung out with one another after dinner. When it was not an organized group fun time, Dante and I acted as buffers between Atticus and Boo until the two of them found a happy equilibrium.

I could give no greater compliment to my brother than to say he was as good a big brother to me as Dante was to Boo.

Always willing to cover for me to Mom and Dad and help me avoid unnecessary punishment, he also often got the task of taking me to various functions like my one and only piano recital. Waiting in the back of the piano teacher's living room crowded with proud parents, Chuck was probably hoping as much as I that it would be over quickly. I had memorized my piece because reading notes was as difficult for me as reading words, and Chuck and I both knew I had it down perfectly except for the one note that his perfect pitch would catch every time I practiced. Even when he was in the family room watching TV, he'd yell out, "B flat! Lisa, it's B flat!" It drove him nuts, but there was no way for me to fix it— it was locked in my muscle memory.

When my turn came, my hands clenched as the teacher put the sheet music in front of me. I could hear the impatient parents shift in their seats uncomfortably. My fingers refused to release, so I tried to play that poor piano with my fists. Creeping out from her kitchen, the teacher hauled me away from the piano, rescuing the stunned audience from the rest of my post-modern interlude.

Chuck quietly collected me for a slow walk home together, as if the speed would allow my shame time to recede before encountering Mom and Dad. In later years, the recollection of Chuck walking me home from my dishonorable defeat at the hands of the piano always reminded me of the scene from *To Kill a Mockingbird* when Jem walks the sad and defeated Scout home, wearing nothing but her underwear and the giant ham costume. I am sure Chuck covered for me and told Mom and Dad (who of course hadn't bothered to attend) that the recital went just fine. He knew that Mom's rage was easily set off by failure or public displays of less-than-perfect behavior.

Chuck had been my protector for as long as I could remember, but never was it more outstanding than on a hot July day when I was almost three years old. My family gathered around a Howard Johnson's poolside table somewhere midway between Illinois and anywhere in Florida, depositing towels, bags, pop, suntan lotion and other sundries. No one noticed the little toddler in the deep end of the pool, blubbering and bobbing up and down with no knowledge of swimming and no hope of climbing out—no one, that is, except my eight-year-old brother, Chuck.

I remember the terror of the water everywhere seeming to press in on me and squeeze me from all sides. I remember my inability to yell and be heard through the chlorine sea that was engulfing me. I remember thinking no one could hear me. I don't recall much after that.

Chuck, as the story goes, saw me in the pool and tried to get an adult's attention, but everyone was so preoccupied with the preswim chaos that they thought he was just doing the old hey-mom-look-at-me thing, and no one listened to him. Taking matters into his own hands, he bravely dove into the ten-foot-deep water to rescue his drowning sister. The commotion of his diving in and splashing around with me in tow finally got the adults' attention, at which point a new form of chaos ensued. Chuck was given the Chocolate-Milk-at-Dinner Award for courage and valor in saving his little sister from drowning. I, however, was given a lifetime fear of water and a debt to my big brother that I had no idea how to repay.

I knew from my own experience just how much a socially happy and healthy individual is shaped in early critical developmental stages, and I took this into account with my three dogs, and Boo in particular.

The story of my birth was such a touchstone for my father that I heard the retelling time and again. I was conceived around the time his father was diagnosed with stomach cancer and given six months to live. Normally, the news of an impending birth would be joyous, but mine was tainted with the impending loss of Grandfather Charlie Sr. and my mother's disinclination to be pregnant again—something she had not wanted.

Upon our return from the hospital, I was greeted by Charlie Sr., who although tired and gaunt from the cancer, spent the day lying on the couch with this new little life. I was only around two days old, so we were both content to sleep through our respective ordeals, me lying on his chest. Charlie told his wife at the end of the day that he just didn't feel well enough to stay overnight as planned.

They left that night, and he died the next day.

My appearance on this planet was ill-timed. For my mother, I showed up at the absolutely worst time, and for my father, I would always be associated with the loss of his father. There was no way for either of them to properly welcome or support this new little life, and this undoubtedly affected my early outlook on life. For example, we know that infants who are cared for by people who are depressed do not typically receive the early neurological stimulation, cognitive or emotional, that is critical to healthy early brain development.

All creatures need to be handled happily and snuggled safely when they're young. It's part of what makes early socializing so important. Studies have shown that touching and snuggling are essential for healthy development in humans and animals alike. When orphaned children in post–World War II Europe were deliberately not touched for fear of infection, they did not develop properly; they lacked appropriate neural pathways, which led to inappropriate social behaviors in later life. Similarly, research has shown that very young puppies who receive early neurological stimulation and positive interactions with humans and other dogs grow to be more confident and adapt better to living with humans. They are also physically healthier and more resilient to the stressors of the human world.

Even when Boo was struggling at home, I worked hard to socialize him with other dogs and in different environments. By the time we adopted Boo, much of his early neurological matrix was setting into place. I had about eight more weeks to give Boo good neurological stimulation through events out and about and good body handling skills in order to give him the best capacity for confidence and learning as he matured. I believe the early socialization experiences that I gave Boo helped shape him into the incredible dog he was to become.

Atticus, Boo and Dante all probably had pretty poor early handling and socialization; however, each of them developed a bit differently. Atticus was always cautious yet confident when around me, but he only loved his inner circle. Boo was slow to learn, with little confidence, and loved everyone and everything with equal passion. Dante was the enigma; despite how sick he was at a young age, he was one of those truly rare dogs who was going to be confident and social no matter what people did to him.

When I took Boo out and about for early socialization, he was always more comfortable when Dante was there with him. Boo, too, probably felt a bit like Scout being supported and taken care of by his big brother, just like I did with Chuck. When Atticus was being too much of a bully with Boo, Dante would walk or run between them, sending each moving in another direction. Moving between the two dogs in this way is a basic canine body language signal called splitting that diffuses tension and eases social pressure between dogs and humans. It is what your dog is attempting to do every time she tries to get between you and someone you are hugging. It isn't that they want to join in the affection but that dogs generally worry when people hug.

Splitting is apparently something humans do, too. Gramma J, my mother's mother who moved in with us when I was almost five, was the only other person in my family I could depend on for emotional support besides Chuck. As my occasional co-conspirator, she often stood between me and Mom and Dad. Gram and I would sneak extra snacks after dinners, she would sign my practice sheets for music lessons (even though I had not practiced) and together we pulled off a family coup d'état in the Kitty Affair. Perhaps she knew I needed a pet of my own, or maybe she just wanted a cat, too. Princess found a wounded cat in the yard and started nursing him back to health, but Dad and Sue were allergic, so we weren't allowed to keep him. Gram and I helped Princess by feeding the cat against strict orders. It wasn't long before the cat was living in the garage, then the basement and then finally in the house as my pet, shared only with Gramma J and Princess, who loved Kitty like her own puppy. Kitty snuggled with me, allowed me to dress him in silly bandanas and gave me the kind of safe physical contact and affection I so desperately needed.

Research at a treatment center for sexually abused children found that bringing friendly pooches into therapy sessions decreased the kids' anxiety as they told their stories for the first time. The pets comforted them so much that when they arrived for the next session, many asked for the dog by name—even though they didn't always remember their therapist's name. My friend Suz Brooks, a Ph.D. and former clinical director at Green Chimneys, speaks often about the ability of animals to help physically and sexually abused children find a safe way to interact physically and learn to touch and be touched again without fear of further abuse. For me, this has played out since the early days of Princess and Kitty.

Ultimately, with help from Dante and guidance from me, Boo began to win over most of his new family. The cats seemed to be working it out well: Tara ignored him, which was perfect for her, and Merlin, although he never truly appreciated Boo's attempts to nibble on his neck as Dante always did, still seemed willing to put up with it. Boo would try his hardest to nibble gently on Merlin, but instead Merlin's entire head ended up in clumsy Boo's mouth. We knew what was going on when Merlin walked by looking disgusted, with all the fur on the top of his head wet and sticking up. Boo wanted to emulate Dante in every way he could, but in many ways, he just wasn't as adept as his big brother. Atticus at least was starting to tolerate Boo and tried to play with him at times. Atticus loved chase, but Boo had trouble getting it quite right. He'd start out chasing Atticus and somehow end up back on the deck racing parallel to Atticus, barking his coyote howl at Atticus, who continued to run back and forth in the yard until he realized the little guy just wasn't getting it.

Yet, Boo still had one more hurdle: Lawrence. Although Lawrence's feelings toward Boo were not as chilly as the weather that December, he wasn't in love with Boo yet either. Lawrence wasn't too thrilled with Boo's slow training progress. Lawrence refused to take part in potty-training and only went out with Boo when I was already out with all the boys. Boo did, however, make Lawrence laugh when he played in the snow, especially as it began to pile up. Snow-blowing the driveway created a mountain of snow in the front yard. Atticus and Dante loved to climb the snow mound and slide down it. Of course, little Boo had to do whatever his brothers did, and one early Sunday morning, he went up the mountain, over the top and down the other side. When he didn't come out, I went to find him, and then I got stuck in the deep drift on the other side of the mountain. When Dante and Atticus returned to the house and stood by the door to be let in without Boo and me, Lawrence got worried and came to investigate. After he stopped laughing at the sight of Boo and me stuck between high mounds of snow, he pulled us both out. Lawrence giggled over this for weeks.

Although Lawrence kept a distance from Boo, he was always a keen observer and occasionally would make statements like, "I worry about that boy. He just ain't right." I dismissed these comments as Lawrence's way of beginning to break down the barriers he put up to keep Boo out—at least he was taking some interest. My hopefulness was supported at times when I'd come home from class and find Lawrence, still recovering from various Crohn's flare-ups, on the couch, asleep on his side, with a little black dog curled up neatly behind his bent knees. Boo was snuggled with Lawrence. Or was it the other way around? When I pressed Lawrence to admit that Boo was growing on him, he assured me that this was the only way he could take a nap and be sure Boo was not getting into trouble.

Lawrence will tell anyone who listens that if it were not for me, he wouldn't have dogs. I know this isn't true because he's the one who brought Dante into our home, and he cannot deny that it was his playing with Atticus that brought us together. To this day, Lawrence claims my first words to him were, "What the hell are you doing to my dog?" He swears it was at that moment that he knew I was his fate.

Six years before Boo came into our lives, I met Lawrence when I was managing Thunder's Mouth Press, a small publisher in SoHo. I was lucky I could bring Atticus to work with me because coming with me to the office was the only real way Atticus was going to get out and about each day. My knees were giving me trouble that no one could explain or fix for years, and by now they were so sore most of the time that my mobility was severely limited. In addition, I developed a very painful, recurring rash that no one could diagnose. Living on 5th Street between Avenues A and B, Atticus and I walked to and from work every day, but by the end of the day, the climb up the five flights of stairs to my apartment usually left me in so much pain that all I could do was cry and put my legs up with ice until bedtime. There were many nights when I simply couldn't take Atticus out for that last pee of the night, and he never moaned or groused; he just waited patiently until morning. I like to believe that he knew I would have taken him out if I could have.

Needing to find a way to get Atticus out during the days turned him into a fixture and sometimes an attraction in our SoHo office. My boss, Neil, was on the fence about having a dog in the office, but Atticus's supporters included the majority of the staff and Anne, the sales manager for our distributor. Whenever Neil raised the possibility of an Atticus-free office, he was outvoted. It was a good thing Neil never knew that Atticus once peed a river in front of Former Secretary of State Ramsey Clark when he was in the office for a meeting. No amount of staff outvoting would have allowed Atticus to stay if that had been revealed. When Atticus was not with me in my private office, I could usually find him in Anne's. She would play with him during her breaks, stroking his fluffy, coarse fur and letting it brush away the stressors of her day. I began to see what a dog could do for spirit, stress and the general well-being of others. Almost every staff member would come to Atticus at some point throughout the day for a moment of canine Zen and stress relief. You could call it my first exposure to animal-assisted therapeutic activities.

In addition to showing me the power of the human–animal bond, Atticus also picked out a husband for me. Not always good with strangers, Atticus nevertheless took to Lawrence right away and was busy playing tug with Lawrence and his baby dino roar when I went looking for him one afternoon in Anne's office and uttered those now-famous words.

I think Lawrence's eyes are his most striking feature. They're a soothing greenish hazel color that's in direct contrast to his scathing wit. With a square build and at five feet ten inches, he's only slightly taller than I am. When I first met him, he was trying desperately to deny his impending baldness with a ponytail made out of a few remaining, lonely locks of hair. He now alternates between a neatly groomed beard that balances the little peach fuzz remaining on the top of his head and a full shave of everything for the Yul Brynner look.

In the corner of my office, I had a big wicker chair that looked like it came from an old plantation, and soon Lawrence was a fixture in that chair, taking his breaks during the day to rotate through the collection of various toys I had scattered around my office, including yo-yos, windup ladybugs, assorted Happy Meal cars and stuffed animals. He would pore over the silly things I had hanging behind my desk on the bulletin board like an archaeologist deciphering hieroglyphs, trying to figure me out.

For about a year, Lawrence spent most of his downtime at work in my office while professing nothing but indifference to me and my dog. Our usual exchanges were replete with abundant sarcasm, witty quips and bawdy humor. On one occasion, he was getting so out of hand with the staff that I stuck my gum in his hair to shut him up. We very much took the mature approach to not being a couple.

Six years later, when I was hoping Lawrence would come to love Boo as I had, I was buoyed a bit thinking about my courtship with Lawrence. I realized that it had taken him time to admit he loved me, so there was hope for Boo with all the boys in our house after all.

3
Training Troubles

It seemed like all Boo had to do to win his place in Lawrence's heart was learn to pee and poop outside. Boo's first winter with us in our dilapidated log house was a terrible one, with a bitter cold that only worsened his potty-training woes. Once the ice began to replace the snow, he didn't want to be out there any more than I did, and when the flu season laid me up for a couple weeks in January, I didn't get Boo out as often as I needed to. The other house-training issues—chewing on contraband items like shoes and the rug upstairs, or Boo's attempt to electrocute himself with the vacuum cleaner's cord—were all much more minor annoyances for Lawrence.

"He's your dog," he would remind me every time I suggested he participate in the freezing potty-training. All Boo's humorous antics in the snow or while chasing the cats could not outweigh the potty issues, and eventually Lawrence began hinting that if the piddling, pooping puppy didn't *get it* soon, he would have to go. My guarded optimism notwithstanding, Lawrence was still in full-out "I-don't-want-Boo" mode.

I needed to move heaven and earth to get Boo trained. He had already been abandoned once, and I was not going to let that happen again. Moreover, Boo was not going to live his life as an outsider in his own family, as I had.

Underlying Lawrence's reluctance was the fact that his medical recovery was just as stalled as Boo's training. Lawrence simply didn't have the energy to reach out to the little guy except in tiny gestures. Lawrence's doctors still hadn't found the right combination of medications to keep him stable enough to avoid multiple flare-ups, and as a result, he was weak and tired all the time. Sometimes these flare-ups were simply annoying for him, and sometimes they were downright life-threatening. One particularly harrowing afternoon at work, he noticed he was bleeding; the doctor insisted that he come in right away. The doctor's office was over an hour away, but I was working in the city that day, so Lawrence had to drive himself. By the time he arrived, he was woozy and pale. The doctors took one look at him, realized he'd lost a dangerous amount of blood and admitted him to the hospital immediately, where he stayed for three days.

The ongoing question of when he would be sick enough to end up in the hospital again made it hard for Lawrence to focus on the little peeing and pooping machine and brought emotional consequences as well. Lawrence became distrustful of intimacy of any kind, emotional or physical, especially when it came to the little puppy, Boo. Having come so close to death and constantly fearing he might face it again at any time, Lawrence developed a powerful fear of losing loved ones, and his response was to distance himself as much as possible from everyone and everything. I felt the sting of this, but Boo the puddle-prone puppy got the brunt of it. From Lawrence's point of view, Boo simply refused to learn his lessons.

Boo, however, kept trying as hard as he could to display his affection for Lawrence. Each evening when Lawrence came home from work, Boo bounded up to him with his happy open mouth, ears flopping and stubby tail wagging in a circle at lightning speed. No matter how clearly Boo's body language said, "I love you," though, he also usually managed to piddle on Lawrence while he was saying it. Any magic that Boo's happy greeting could have conjured to win over Lawrence was literally pissed away. Tired of being peed on every evening when he came home, and nightly cleaning up of various other "mistakes," Lawrence eventually stopped hinting and began overtly suggesting that we give Boo away.

It became a familiar scene in our home in those months. Lawrence usually began, "Damnit, these are my work pants," then continued, "He can't control himself. Hell, he doesn't even know where the doors are. He just wanders around the house."

Seeing Lawrence upset and angry, Boo usually slunk away and disappeared into the background to hide until things quieted down.

Lawrence continued the tirade: "Other people wouldn't put up with this, and he'd have been dropped off at a shelter by now. I don't see why we have to put up with it."

I tried to explain by saying, "He's still learning. Every dog learns at their own pace, and we have to support him."

Yet, my reasoning did nothing to help Lawrence muster the strength, interest or patience to assist Boo with his potty-training. Every night ended with Lawrence saying, "This has to stop soon, or we have to find him another house."

I was in tears much of the time, blaming myself for bringing this confused little puppy into a home where he was not fully wanted, where I struggled to get him to learn faster. It broke my heart to think of losing Boo, and I was starting to resent Lawrence for not wanting him.

I couldn't make Lawrence love Boo. Only Boo could make Lawrence love Boo. But to get Boo to the place where he could do that, he needed confidence and to learn how to live in a world outlined by the social mores of humans. It had taken *me years* to develop confidence and a rudimentary understanding of life skills. Boo didn't have years.

When I left home at seventeen to start college at Western Illinois University, it was the only choice I could make. At the time, I was engaged to a junior there who insisted I go to the same school, so I went to the same school. Mom, in an amazing moment of clarity, even altruism, immediately signed me up for a study-abroad program for my second semester (to get me away from my fiancé). It worked, and the transatlantic breakup left me free to follow another man to the University of Illinois at Urbana-Champaign. I had been in the pre-law track at Western, probably subconsciously hoping to right wrongs by using the legal system to "fix things" (I still thought justice worked like it did in Frank Capra movies), but the pre-law track at UIUC was much tougher than at Western, and the reading was killing me. After several unsuccessful attempts to get help, I was sent to a specialist.

Following days of testing, Dr. Maglione explained that the reason I had difficulty reading was because I was dyslexic. At nineteen years old, I had never heard this term before. He said I was actually pretty smart (I scored well on the IQ test), but the dyslexia would always get in my way. He suggested I would probably be good at design, art or even creative writing with one of the newfangled computer programs that helped with spelling. Dr. Maglione also explained that I would never be a good reader—my shopping lists attest to that ("lettus, brocolie," etc.)—but little by little, over the years, my reading has gotten a little better. Not too different from Atticus, who learned his "down" command at age nine. You *can* teach an old dog new tricks; they won't be perfect, but they'll still enrich the dog's life.

A final piece of irony was that Dr. Maglione and my father were in graduate school together ("You look just like your mother" was the first thing he said to me when I walked into his office). I suspect the doctor did not call every testing student's father after the test results were in and rebuke him for being an educator who let his daughter flounder for so many years without appropriate help. My mother, trying to justify this, explained to me that Dad had been worried about how it would look if the superintendent's daughter was thought to be "retarded." In order to keep up appearances, my parents decided not to tell anyone I was dyslexic, and they hoped I would "grow out of it."

After the testing, I left for New York City to be an artist and eventually began a career as a bohemian photomontage artist. I had a couple shows, and people seemed to like my work, but I lacked the self-assurance to hawk myself to galleries. I managed, through happenstance, to land a job as a political photographer in state politics. This gave me stability, a steady income, an expense account and the opportunity to be goosed by Hunter S. Thompson at the Democratic National Convention (my boyfriend at the time managed to parlay an autograph from Thompson as an apology). I went to fundraisers, state hearings, political functions and then home every day to my tiny closet of a studio in the East Village (long before it was trendy) that I shared with my cat, Clousseau.

Like Boo, I was trying very hard to be the best I could in my new situation. And like Boo, my ability to mess things up stayed with me no matter how hard I tried, to similar, unexpected, comical effects. I was given thirty seconds to photograph the governor of New York State with a State Senate candidate. On lookout in City Hall Park, I jumped down from the stands where I had been perched and landed directly in front of the governor. As I motioned for the candidate to join us, I saw the governor's bodyguards reach for their weapons.

"Governor," I said, "you remember Andy, running for the State Senate? We just need a picture of you two together." I got no response. Moving to stand next to Andy, the governor looked like he wished his guards would just shoot me. I said, "Please . . . you and Andy are supposed to be friends." There was no change in their sour demeanors. "Buddies," I said, and at this point it looked like everyone was in agreement that someone should get shot, "I need a smile! You're supposed to be &%^$% paisans. For the *^&%^ love of God, could somebody give me a !#$@# smile?"

After the string of expletives, the governor's face started to crack, and he clutched Andy in a tremendous shoulder hug, just as his smile reached from ear to ear. The security men tried to hide their smirks as they holstered their guns. After the picture, the governor grabbed my hand and said, "That was great."

I was doing the best I could, hoping that would be enough, but sometimes in the darker days of my life in the late eighties, trying to make it in New York, it felt like nothing would go right as I struggled to fit in somewhere. I managed to break an old, unhealthy habit of dating multiple guys at the same time, but I was still repeating other old dysfunctional patterns. I was desperately in love with a man named Prescott, hoping to spend the rest of my life with him. One day he would be infatuated with me and write me gooey love letters that would melt the most cynical of hearts. The next day he would remember he was ashamed of me for not being wealthy enough for his family, not Harvard educated, or not Jewish. He would tell me he couldn't admit our relationship to his friends and would withdraw all his protestations of love. This hurtful pattern awakened deeper wounds of mine. It cut too close to the pain created by the sexual abuse I suffered as a child. It followed the same pattern of dysfunctional "love" followed by shunning, withdrawal, and feelings of shame and guilt. In my heart, it didn't matter if my father was telling me, "Tell no one. It would hurt your mother," or if Prescott was telling me, "I'm not ready to let you meet my friends," or "You can't come visit us in the country because my father doesn't like you." In both instances, I was being rejected by a family in which I desperately wanted to belong, and I was the one expected to carry the guilt and responsibility for Prescott's and my father's actions. All I could see looming was a lifetime of repeating these dysfunctional relationships, only to be shunned and rejected no matter how hard I tried to fit in and make it right.

Finally, after Prescott spent my birthday with his family but left me in the city because his father said, "I don't want that woman in my house," I treated myself to a nice dinner, went home, opened a bottle of wine, left a few goodbye messages with friends and turned the stove pilot light off.

My suicide attempt took a while—I suspect because I left the window open a tiny crack so the cat would be able to squeeze back in after I was gone—and thanks to two ex-boyfriends who were concerned by the messages I left them, I was whisked to the hospital just in time. I was locked in the "loony bin," as my mother would have put it, for the New York State's mandatory seventy-two-hour hold, but in reality, this was the beginning of the long dark trek toward sanity. No one visited except for Prescott's sister, who was sympathetic, but it gave another reason for his parents to further reject me and think I wasn't good enough for their son. I never told my family, as I knew this would have become another reason for them to tease and denigrate me, and firmly believing the rest of the world would be as harsh as my family, I never told most of my friends either.

After being released from the hospital I went back to my tiny apartment and my cat. Without support from friends (who thought I had just been sick for those three days) or professionals (I didn't put too much stock in psychology at the time), I did my best to keep a positive attitude, but Prescott was still there, and my family was still looming. At least I realized suicide was not the answer and struggled to find another external solution. Traveling to London had gotten me out of a bad high school engagement, so perhaps traveling farther—halfway around the world—would break me of this horrible cycle of wanting to be accepted by people who never would.

I went to India to see an old college friend, but on a side trip to Kathmandu, I wound up lying passed out in my own vomit, half concussed from the blow to my head that happened on the "way down." Crawling through the multiple puddles of vomit to the phone, I called for help. I had no idea how I'd gotten to the floor, what had made me sick or how sick I actually was. When the concierge arrived, he tucked me into bed, called a doctor and sat staring at me with a look that crossed the language barrier and clearly said, "Please don't die on my shift."

I managed to literally get the very last seat on a plane out of New Delhi before the new year and made it back to New York for Christmas Eve. Prescott swore he would meet me at the airport, but he never showed.

All I could think to do was go back to *my* family and, hoping for a miracle, try again. Still sick from Kathmandu, I booked a flight to Chicago on Christmas Day. When I called from the airport, Dad said, "Who the hell do you think is going to come pick you up on Christmas Day?"

It turned out to be just like other typical family Christmases. Dad and I had not been speaking for almost five years at that point, save for a few grunts of hello. When I asked my sister and brother-in-law if they wanted to get together while I was home, they told me they were too busy. On the bright side, Chuck was still in graduate school, so he would often be home for the same few days I was, and we would have our usual holiday movie festivals and do some tree trimming.

The second day into that visit, I had a 104-degree temperature and couldn't move. The doctor diagnosed Campylobacter jejuni (a bacterial infection much like cholera), so at least we knew what made me so sick in Kathmandu. They gave me massive amounts of antibiotics, and I retreated back to New York City.

Life gives us recurring messages until we learn whatever it is we are supposed to learn—not unlike poor dog trainers who repeat their commands over and over again until the dog simply guesses or gets lucky. I could not even begin to guess what I was supposed to learn from the repeated messages of being continually unwanted—by my family and by Prescott's. I was like the dog struggling to understand: Should I put my butt on the floor to make the choking stop? Should I lay down to make the choking stop? Should I bark, jump up, roll over—what, what will make the choking stop?

I finally gave up on Prescott, although it took

74

another year and a half until I finally gave him an ultimatum: commit or get out. He got out, and within the space of about six months in the late 1980s, I quit the Senate, started dating other men and began waiting tables at the Cedar Tavern in Greenwich Village. It was the perfect place for me to be surrounded by the old familiar dysfunction of drinking and drunkenness. A beautiful, dark, old wooden bar from the forties, it boasted a heritage of serving until drunk and passed out, a number of the members of the New York school of abstract expressionism: Jackson Pollack, Jasper Johns, Franz Kline and a few others.

I was back to being a bohemian artist on the Lower East Side. I worked on my photomontages daily before going to wait tables at night; I amassed almost three dozen pieces during that time. After the suicide attempt, I was ordered to undergo therapy, but I didn't stay with it for long because of an ingrained family belief that therapy was for crazy people. The real reason I left therapy, I'm sure, was that the memories were just too painful. My photomontages were filled with images of confinement, dark shadows, women being used and abused, all cut by light streaking across other images like a knife. The art had become my therapy.

Clearly it wasn't enough. It was almost three years after the suicide attempt before I was back into my old patterns, spiraling from one boy-friend to another. Three more relationships, a brief, badly broken engagement, and I found myself in another dark place that was too close to the edge. I stopped drinking alcohol after my suicide attempt, but even without drinking, I was near the precipice again.

I called an ex-boyfriend who was still close to me. When he understood how bad things were, he got worried and came by with a tarot deck to distract me. He opened up a door for me that night for which I will forever be grateful. I don't usually remember my dreams, but I remembered the one from that night. In my dream I was at home in the family room with Gramma J, who had passed away five years before. The room was bright, brighter than it had ever been. She was making her usual Sanka in her favorite, old, stained cup and was exactly as I always remembered her: glowing, smooth, porcelain cheeks with shocking white hair and a mischievous smile. Stirring her Sanka, she said to me, "It'll be okay."

It had been three years since the last time I *thought* I needed to go home. When I woke up, I had an overwhelming urge to go home again.

This time, not only did Mom and Dad pick me up at the airport, but they also actually met me inside at baggage claim, which had always been too much of a burden for them before. It still makes me tear up to think about it—that act was so dramatically different from their usual behavior. Dad was quiet on the ride home—no insults, no interrogations, nothing. When I walked into the house from the garage, the light in the room was exactly like it was in my dream. The chills up my spine stopped me dead in my tracks. "It's so bright," I said.

"We just put in new fans with brighter lights a week ago," Mom explained.

For the first and only time in my life, I told Mom about the whirlwind of dating trouble I was having. She was practically sympathetic and obviously relayed this information to Dad. He had been in recovery for almost a year at that point, and while Mom had given up on the Al-Anon meetings, Dad was still very much working his AA program.

At one point, when all was pretty quiet in the house, Dad came to talk to me. "Lees," he said, "I have been going to meetings. It's helped me a lot. There are meetings for family members of alcoholics, too."

I was waiting for the insult, the judgment, the punishment, but they didn't come. Instead, he said, "I did some things to you that you may not remember very well. You have probably tried to hide them."

I felt a cold shudder all through my body, wrapped my arms tightly across my chest as I started to shiver and felt myself at the edge of hyperventilating. The flash of my bedroom and the light streaming in from the hallway pulled at me as if his words opened the door to those memories. My grabbing and holding onto myself was my attempt to shut that door again, but it couldn't be shut. "You might want to consider going to some Al-Anon meetings," he continued. What was to be gained by going to some meetings? I wasn't sure about any of this, but what I did know was that this was not my father of old who was talking to me. He really did seem to care. He knew better than to try to touch or hug me for the entire trip. This beginning of repentance and suggestion of where to begin to get help was the greatest gift he ever gave me.

I gave Al-Anon a try and found many people struggling with their own addictions or, like me, the fallout from the addictions of family members. Rob and I had been friendly since before I worked for the State Senate. We kept in touch as friends, and ironically he was just beginning his recovery work in AA as I started Al-Anon. Although we broke one of the *Big Book* rules and started dating as we both began our recoveries, we ended up supporting each other through this period that took us up to Albany for a year, then back to New York City where Rob brought Atticus into our lives. That was when I truly began to rebuild my personal foundation and learn what unconditional love was.

As the first being who accepted me unconditionally, Atticus was the universe's way of throwing me a lifeline. He taught me how to let myself be accepted by those who would and, when not accepted, to not care. Without him, my recovery would have plateaued somewhere in the middle of a dark place. Atticus also brought me to the dogs. Without Atticus, there would have been no high point to my recovery, no Dante, and no Boo.

It was easy to see from my own past how Lawrence was just displacing his daily frustrations onto Boo. Regardless of all my efforts, I did not know how to help Lawrence be more patient with the four-and-a-half-month-old Boo. Although it isn't unusual for a twenty-week-old dog to still be working through some potty-training issues, there are usually some indicators that the dog is beginning to get it. Boo showed no indication of getting it.

"It's like he's doing it out of spite," Lawrence said once.

"Boo is not making these mistakes out of spite," I said. "He just needs extra guidance, acceptance and patience."

"Well, can't we speed his learning up?"

Trying to deflect to something amusing and

change the topic, I said, "If Atticus could pee in front of Ramsey Clark, then what are some piddles around the house while Boo is learning?"

But nothing lightened the mood in the house, and Lawrence just said, "Boo ain't no Atticus."

I cried repeatedly into Boo's soft, thick fur, hoping I could make him wanted in his own home. Lawrence loved Atticus and Dante with all his heart, but poor little Boo just couldn't seem to do anything right. That struck me deep to the core. Boo had to be house-trained so Lawrence could focus on what was really frustrating him: his own medical condition.

I knew all too well the toll that medical conditions could take. I knew Lawrence was in pain, frustrated, angry and probably scared. I went through all of these years before as my joint pain had become severe enough to make sitting through a two-hour film so painful that I cried at the end of every movie I went to, even action thrillers. My social life was limited, my dog's life was limited and it seemed like nothing would be normal again. Every night as I climbed up my loft stairs where Tara, Merlin and I would snuggle for the night, leaving Atticus staring up at me from the couch, I promised him that somehow I'd find an apartment I could afford with an elevator and room for a bed that he could share with me and the cats. I knew he had no clue what I was saying when I made him this promise, but it made me feel better because every time he would tilt his head in the same way he would when I asked if he wanted a "cookie." He liked something about what I was saying. For years, my existence was defined by the limitations of pain and other symptoms: I had skin disorders, dry eyes, dry nasal passages and dry mouth, and my fingers turned white and numb for no good reason.

Although my diagnosis was always changing depending on the doctor I was seeing—mixed connective tissue disorder, lupus, overlap syndrome, fibromyalgia and laughably chronic double-jointedness—Lawrence had a definitive diagnosis, and while this offered a modicum of relief to know the exact problem, there was still the long struggle of developing the right treatment plan and learning to manage a chronic condition. I knew exactly how he felt, and I'm not sure I would have made it through those painful years in New York without the comfort of Atticus, Tara and Merlin. Atticus was there for me—always and without judgment. Looking back, I can see how important these animals were for maintaining my health, sanity and social skills. On so many levels, Atticus demonstrated the essential benefits of the dynamic human–animal bond. I didn't realize it at the time, but he was teaching me a powerful lesson about animal-assisted therapy.

Seeing how uncomfortable Lawrence was, I couldn't help but think that if he would just open up to little Boo, he might start to feel better—to even heal faster. If only he would warm up to the little fellow.

Part of the reason I was so anxious for Lawrence to warm up to Boo was that of all the dogs, I was most like Boo, with our parallel lack of confidence and slow learning. As a result, I was continually turning inward to avoid judgment. It was this fear that kept me from ever going through a formal job search—I was always just in the right (or sometimes wrong) place at the right (or sometimes wrong) time. When it was time to leave Thunder's Mouth Press, I was terrified of the prospect of job hunting, but once again luck intervened, and I managed to get a job through a friend of a friend whose friend had just bought a literary agency and needed someone to manage the office. I needed a job, and there was one looking me in the face. The agency had been through an earthquake of transition that left the office buried so deep in piles of paper that I had to work six days a week to get things organized. This was the first time since Atticus came into my life that I didn't have him at my side throughout the day for support. Apparently I was ready to be on my own.

Busy cleaning house at the agency and setting up my new apartment (with an elevator), I had no time to think about a relationship until a year after Atticus introduced me to Lawrence. The delay worked out well for us. Lawrence was recovering from his own bad relationship and wasn't convinced that he could risk such heartbreak again. Meanwhile, I was about as gun-shy about relationships as one could get and had finally accepted that I probably would end up being the crazy, spinsterish dog lady of 9th Street. We both had to take a leap of faith and step out of our comfort zones. We began flirting over e-mail, then we figured we'd try to have some face-to-face time. Within another year, we were married.

Our similarly twisted senses of humor and sarcasm worked to bring us together while simultaneously driving us apart. Knowing how tough it would be for us to have a reasonably normal relationship with our respective baggage, we entered couples therapy within the first year of marriage. I'm certain that's why we're still married, fifteen years later. When our therapist asked us to dispense with sarcasm for a month, we couldn't find anything to say to each other for a week. We eventually succeeded, even though the next three weeks weren't easy. We can make each other laugh, and we each understand what it is like to be afraid.

Lawrence's biological father was brutal to him and his mother, and after his parents divorced, Lawrence lived with him, enduring the ongoing brutality for a couple more years. Lawrence rebelled and eventually was put onto a plane to Florida to live with his mother and stepfather. I believe Lawrence's defiance saved his life because life with his mother and stepfather was a happy and supportive time that brought him no physical harm. He has always referred to his stepfather as his father and almost never mentions his biological father.

Lawrence and I are excellent examples of the fallout of punishment and abuse. He's the dog who will fight back when being hung from a choke chain or shocked; I'm like the dog who simply shuts down and curls up, hoping to go unnoticed. We each spent time unlearning the dysfunctional ways that were taught to us as children, and we each knew all too well what harsh or inappropriate treatment can do to one's abilities to trust and joyfully partake in life. I reminded Lawrence of this time and again when he became vexed with Boo and started to yell. We all yell at some point in our lives at loved ones, but yelling is not training. We have to listen to ourselves when we are teaching others—people or dogs—and if we are only yelling or stern, we forget our own humanity.

Lawrence and I were living on 9th Street and

Broadway, the epicenter of NYU student partying on the weekends. With only Atticus, it was easy to avoid the students—out for a quick pee, and Atticus would want to get back inside. But once Dante came into our lives, the Friday and Saturday late-night walks were taken over by drunken NYU students.

"Wow, thashs a big dog," a student would slur all over Lawrence, or "Doeshs that dog bite? Heh, heh, heh." Each weekend evening I would wait, biting my lip, for Lawrence to return with the gory tales of the verbal thrashings he had offered the inebriated while out with the dogs, and eventually he began making noises about leaving the city.

Two episodes finally pushed us to leave my newly renovated, cozy apartment. One afternoon at the dog run, I tried to get Dante to wait calmly in the entry pen, but the best he could do in his excitement was a sort of hover-sit, where his butt hovered just over the ground like a race car revving its engines. Giving up, I opened the gate, and Dante launched into the air, flying over two people seated on a park bench.

I watched, screaming, "Noooooo!" Or maybe it was, "Look oooooout!" The two people on the bench in Dante's low-fly zone looked up as the huge dog, with his boy bits and tail flapping in the breeze, just grazed their heads.

Laughing at that, Lawrence observed, "That

dog needs more room to run." I agreed but didn't want to leave the city.

The straw that broke the camel's back came one night when Dante broke out of his collar and ran loose down 9th Street—in the middle of the Holland Tunnel traffic. Lawrence scooped Atticus up midpoop and took off after Dante. Weaving through the traffic, Dante led Lawrence into the middle of 9th Street still carrying the shocked and confused white dog. A doorman from the building on the corner of 9th and University tried to clothesline Dante but ended up flat on his back. Lawrence shouted an apology as he ran by, Atticus still flying on his shoulder. Moving west across University Place, Lawrence lost sight of Dante as his tail seemed to be clipped by a bus. Lawrence finally caught up to him in front of the grocery store and was able to plant himself in Dante's path. All three of them landed just outside the door of Gristedes—a two dog/one human pileup.

(Years later when Lawrence would be frustrated with Boo, I would remind him that Dante had some rough edges in the beginning. Lawrence would counter by saying, "Yeah, but he was house-trained in a month.")

Lawrence pushed to leave the city, and I dug my heels in until he hit on the one point with which I could not argue: Atticus was aging. He was almost nine, and because he recovered just a few months earlier from an almost fatal illness, we were keenly aware of his mortality. The first promise I made to Atticus was to give him a home where he could go out whenever he needed to, where his outings were not at the whim of my painful knees and where he could sleep in the bed next to me. The 9th Street apartment had fulfilled that promise. The second promise I had made to him was that he would one day have a grassy area to play—9th Street couldn't offer him that.

Online we found a rundown log house in Putnam County. It was in our price range but much farther from the city than I had hoped; we would both be commuting on the train. I absolutely hated the house; everything had a poorly stained or completely unfinished wood surface. But we ultimately had only two months to make a contract, close the deal and move, so with no other choice, we bought it.

The first time I took Atticus and Dante out for a pee at the new house, they didn't know what to do with all that grass. When I suggested they just pee on the green stuff, they looked at me as if it were a setup—an episode of Canine Candid Camera, perhaps?

Lawrence's concern about Atticus's need for a country place to retire was not completely self-serving. He loved Atticus and Dante as much as I did, worried when they were sick and took them to the dog parks in spite of his distaste for interacting with that many people at one time. When we took a trip to Paris, he missed them so much that he wrote songs about them. Perhaps it was the locale that made him think back to his college days in Paris when he co-opted the tune to Edith Piaf's "Milord" for "Who Are My Two Puppies?":

> Who are my two puppies?
> That would be Attapooch,
> And with his brother Dante,
> They're two big goofs.
>
> They like to run and play.
> They like to bark all day.
> But when they get sleepy,
> They can't stay awake.
>
> They like to chase the cats
> To give 'em heart attacks,
> But when bedtime comes,
> They're two big bed hogs . . .

How could the man who sang songs about his dogs through the streets of Paris not warm up to Boo? I just had to have faith.

We moved in July, and by the end of August, I found what I had spent over a year looking for in New York City. I had seen what Atticus could do for other people's emotional states at work and for mine at home. Now I had Dante, the friendliest, goofiest dog in the world, who loved everyone he met. I knew he'd be perfect as a visiting dog, and here it was, in the PennySaver in Putnam County of all places, an ad for an animal-assisted therapy class starting in Mahopac. I signed us up immediately.

Dante was ebullient and happy but completely untrained. He sat after a couple repeated commands and walked pretty well on leash, but those skills barely cracked the surface of what he needed to go visiting. Luckily for me, Dante was a fast learner; I had to work to keep up with him. Testing day came, and in spite of all the progress we'd made, we failed miserably. I was in tears, and Dante was shaking at my side, feeding off my stress. The woman who organized the class, Diane Pennington, was just starting an organization called H.A.R.T. Programs (Human–Animal Relational Therapies). She was committed to increasing the number of visiting teams and took pity on me. She offered some suggestions, met with me once or twice, and I read everything I could find while we practiced. I offered to help Diane with the next class in exchange for her letting Dante and me participate without a fee. She agreed, and my training career was born.

Teaching an animal-assisted therapy class was

an odd way to start a dog-training career. I didn't realize it then, but animal-assisted therapy training is the college level of dog training. When the class finished, Dante and I were up for our second round of testing. We passed. The evaluator, amazed at the progress we'd made since our last test, went so far as to tell me I had a knack.

At last I had the words to describe what Atticus did for me and what I hoped Dante could do for others: animal-assisted therapeutic activities through the human–animal bond. In March of 2000, Dante and I began visiting with adults with developmental disabilities.

But a year later, in March of 2001, after Dante's glorious triumph over the Pet Partners' (formerly Delta Society) evaluation, I was convinced that I was the worst trainer in the world because I still couldn't get my six-month-old puppy to stop peeing and pooping in the house. I was struggling on every level to find Boo acceptance in his own home, to find a way to help him learn and to know what Boo was here to teach me.

4

Something for Chuck

Boo improved just a tiny bit each day
in those first four months, and despite Lawrence's
reservations, I could see him warming up to the
little guy bit by bit. At the same time, that hard,
horrible winter started Boo and me on an
amazing journey, born of a desire to help both
Boo and my brother.

After so many years of feeling like the outsider
in my own family, I finally began moving to a
reasonable place of peace in my relationship
with Mom and Dad. Although Dad and I had not
discussed the abuse again, his behavior—180
degrees from what it had been—spoke more to
me than any apology. We could avoid sticky
subjects by sticking to our common ground. I
was always building something around the
house, and Dad was the consummate weekend
builder. He understood and appreciated my
stories of thirty stringers hand-cut for the deck
stairs. Mom, as always, went along and was
interested in whatever interested Dad. Her focus
on the perfect softened a bit with age, and she
was starting to be able to laugh at the imperfect
things about us all, even herself.

The rest of the family was a work in progress.

Over the years, I didn't feel safe around my family, so I shut down much of the communication from my end. I hoped for a while to repair the rift between my sister and me, but nothing ever came of my efforts. Many years later, I realized how futile that hope was when, screaming and cursing at me over the phone, she let slip the feelings I always suspected she had. "You are not a part of this family," she said, letting each word dig into me like a weapon. "You left this family years ago. You have never been a part of this family."

I am always struck by the power of dogs to forgive. When Atticus and I split from Rob, six years went by before Atticus saw him again—half of Atticus's life had gone by, yet when Rob and his wife and children came for a visit, Atticus squealed with delight and reverted to puppy happiness at the sight and smell of Rob. Like Argos, the dog in the *Odyssey* who remembers his master after he returns from his twenty-year journey, it was clear that Atticus never forgot Rob and forgave him immediately for his long absence.

I got lucky and found that Chuck was more like Argos than my sister. Although he and I had drifted apart and didn't speak much save for holiday visits, there were a few times in those years when the holiday chaos was quiet, and we'd have a conversation that brought back some of the old feelings of comfort that we'd once had with each other. Once his daughter was born, that comfort seemed to grow, and we'd spend more time together during the holidays than before, always making sure to take my niece out for a treat. Thanks to family gatherings and celebrations, our relationship deepened in the six months after Lawrence and I got married. My old comfort with Chuck was restored, and I was thrilled.

Chuck and I started to speak more often on the phone and then by e-mail, which allowed us to check in more frequently. All was well until about a year and a half after Lawrence and I were married. I was on the phone with Chuck and his wife one Sunday afternoon when I noticed that he was slurring his words. I immediately wondered if he had been drinking, but then I realized that the signs I had become so familiar with over the years weren't there. He was in complete control of himself, just not in control of his *speech*. His emotions were on an even keel, and his wife didn't have any of the tension in her voice that had always been there when Mom tried to laugh away my father's drinking. My niece was on the phone, too, and she wasn't *acting* as if she were okay, the way we all used to—she really *was* okay. Chuck was talkative, whereas when Dad was drinking, he would usually be terse, stilted or insulting. I couldn't very well ask what was wrong (in my family, you could have blood spurting out the top of your head during family dinner, and it would be considered inappropriate to ask, "Are you all right?"), so I simply filed the information away and hoped to collect more.

In the meantime, Chuck told me that he'd decided to go back to school to become a CPA. He already had a master's degree in organic chemistry, but he felt that being an accountant would give him more career options. He and his wife were working in a veterans' hospital—she was a head administrative nurse, and he worked in the general hospital administration—and a CPA job would mean better pay and insurance. Since he was very mathematically inclined, I thought he'd be very good at it. Remember, he was the guy who could whoop me in a game of chess during commercial breaks and correct my piano playing from the other room. We talked about the classes he was taking and the tests he would have to pass. I was very happy for him. He seemed so eager, and things seemed to be on a nice track for him. His family was doing well, he was moving ahead with his career goals, he was growing tomatoes in his garden from seeds, and now that he had Dad's old radial saw, he was doing some woodworking again. This hobby was another thing that Chuck and I had in common, probably because he had the same experience with Dad's woodworking as I did. The only place I ever felt safe with Dad as a kid was when he was doing a woodworking project among power tools and other sharp objects. He was always sober when he was doing his woodworking.

But as the months went by, Mom's and Dad's voices began to change dramatically when they talked about Chuck, his family or anything regarding his future. Either they were really pissed at him for something I'd never know about, or they were worried. The next time I saw Chuck—when Boo was still about four months old—it was clear that something was wrong.

In stature, Chuck had always resembled Mom's Swedish-German brothers—tall, lanky and broad. He'd dabbled in basketball and done well at track and field in his high school days, preferring sprinting and the long jump. In the seventies, when he wore his hair long and shaggy and coupled it with a longish mustache, he looked like a strong, healthy forty-niner about to strike gold. That devil-may-care look of the olde-tyme gold miner carried him through college, grad school and lab work. When he started working a more managerial office job at the hospital, his hair and mustache were both trimmed neatly, but he was still physically imposing.

On this visit, however, I was shocked to see how much weight he'd lost. His speech was still slurring, and now his movement was halting and awkward at times. Family decorum kept me from asking about anything, but finally, after I'd gotten back home, I was on the phone with Mom and Dad and realized that there was really nothing they could do if I asked an "inappropriate" question, so I did.

"Is Chuck okay?"

They hesitated to answer. Then, finally, Dad spoke. "There's something wrong with him, but they're not sure what it is yet." I could tell that Mom wanted to keep the secret, but Dad continued, "They think it's either multiple sclerosis or ALS."

I was silent.

"It stands for amyotropic lateral sclerosis, or Lou Gehrig's disease."

We were supposed to be a very formal family and hide emotions, but I had never been adept at burying feelings, so I just stammered, "How long? When did he. . . ." It was an incoherent jumble as I tried to wrap my head around the reality. There were no words I could have said that would convey the stunned sadness that washed over me.

I knew what multiple sclerosis could do and what it ultimately would look like. My grandmother's stepson, Eddie, had MS. He spent the latter half of his life in a wheelchair, with limited ability to navigate even the electronic controls of his own chair. He had to be fed by hand and later through a feeding tube. Each night he had to be mechanically hoisted from his wheelchair into his bed. This disease was bad enough, but then I investigated ALS.

I had heard about ALS before but only from the movie *The Pride of the Yankees* (the Lou Gehrig story was, ironically, one of Chuck's and my favorite old movies). The disease affects the nerve cells in the brain and spinal cord that control voluntary muscle movement, causing them to waste away or die, which means that the muscles can no longer receive messages to do the everyday things we normally take for granted. The individual slowly loses the ability to move hands, arms, legs, and the muscles involving speech, swallowing and breathing, and eventually the whole body is affected. Finally, when the muscles stop getting signals from the nerves to initiate movement, they atrophy. When the muscles in the chest stop receiving input and no longer function, it becomes hard or impossible to breathe without assistance. ALS doesn't affect the senses—sight, smell, taste, hearing and touch—or a person's ability to think or reason. Typically, death occurs within three to five years of diagnosis, but about a quarter of people with ALS survive for more than five years after the appearance of initial symptoms.

I was devastated after I finished my research. It

sounded like drowning alive! The irony shook me, and I was taken back to the early images of my own near drowning that came back to me in frightening black-and-white, shattered recollections.

I wanted some hope for the brother who had saved my life in so many ways. I *decided* to hope that it would turn out to be MS—the lesser of two evils. After all, there had been tremendous breakthroughs for MS since Eddie died in the seventies. But if it turned out to be ALS, I had to hope there were new medications and new treatments, and I had to remind myself that Stephen Hawking has lived for years with ALS. For over a year, hope hung in the air like an ominous balloon.

My parents continued to give me more details in dribbles, and when Chuck learned that I knew, he gave me more bits and pieces—never much specific information, just comments about supplements, experimental meds and testing. There is no single diagnostic test for ALS. Individuals have to undergo a series of tests to rule out other possible diseases. Only after they tested Chuck for everything else and watched the progression of symptoms would they know for certain. He went through one test after another, always hoping *this* would be the test that would deliver bad but not horrible news, only to be told to take another test, and another, and another.

After what seemed like an eternity of waiting and wondering what the ultimate diagnosis would be, all other possibilities were finally ruled out. My brother had Lou Gehrig's disease.

As the disease continued its slow but sure advance, with loss of mobility creeping into his list of symptoms, Chuck continued working as long as he could, even after he almost completely lost his ability to speak. Every day he would take the stairs instead of the elevator up to his office to exercise his weakening muscles. On the weekends, he did his best to continue his woodworking on Dad's old radial saw, tend his garden and spend time with his family. I assume this is the old Protestant work ethic in play—it can be a curse, but I suspect Chuck's inherited obstinacy added a little time to his life.

My times with Chuck after his diagnosis had moments of joy. One Christmas when I was visiting him and his family, the topic of baseball came up. I had come to loathe sports as a kid. Games were always on our TV all day Sunday, the day Dad drank the most—the day I dreaded the most. Regardless, I have a soft spot for the Cubs, cultivated by our annual trips to Wrigley Field and solidified forever on April 16, 1972, the day of the Cubs' famous no-hitter pitched by Burt Hooton. The season started late that year because of a baseball strike, and Wrigley Field was packed to overflowing with eager fans. I bet there were forty thousand fans in the stadium; Mom and Chuck laughed at my guess, pointing out that the stadium held only thirty-nine thousand people. They were shocked at my intuition when Jack Brickhouse announced a record turnout of over thirty-nine thousand fans. Ah, to be young, naive and a good guesser!

The game went on as usual for a while, but then I started getting confused. Each pop fly or catcher-caught foul ball would rock the stands, bringing the fans to their feet with the kinds of cheers usually reserved for home runs and triple plays. I asked what was going on; as Mom was about to explain, Chuck elbowed her so hard in the ribs that he probably bruised a couple.

"Mom! You don't *ever* call a game until the last out of the ninth inning is on the board!"

She remembered standard Cubs paranoia and told me, "Your brother is right. You'll have to wait."

For Chuck that game was the event of a lifetime, and so it was for me, too. He carefully inscribed his scorecard, tracking each out for the opposing team and each hit and run for the Cubs to the very last pitch.

Reminiscing that Christmas after his diagnosis, Chuck obviously had to struggle to get himself up by sheer force of will to retrieve that scorecard. I remember tears welling up when he produced that old piece of cardstock—he knew *exactly* where it was. The expression on his face, the look in his eyes and his body language said what he couldn't say out loud anymore. He handled the scorecard as if it were a holy relic, and when he handed it to me, I too held it like a cherished icon. We had shared an amazing day in 1972, and I was thankful that we were able to share it again.

At home, meanwhile, Dante and I were quite prolific in our therapeutic visits, and I became the deputy director of H.A.R.T. Programs, the nonprofit animal-assisted therapy organization that originally led us into the work. While training for H.A.R.T., I worked closely with founder/director Diane Pennington, and we often touched base with her mentor, Susan, who had been doing animal-assisted therapy in pediatric oncology units for years. Susan was my first trainer with Dante, and in addition to preparing dogs for therapeutic activities, she also trained several service dogs per year for her own nonprofit organization. As I was starting to hear more and more about service dogs, H.A.R.T. recruited a number of teams for Guiding Eyes for the Blind, breeding dogs, released dogs and puppies still in training, and I became friendly with many of them. Because of these relationships, everywhere I turned was as if the universe was throwing up a blinking light saying, "Service dog! Service dog! Service dog!"

I was also becoming more aware that service dogs were no longer just limited to being guide dogs for people with visual disabilities. They could also be hearing alert dogs, seizure alert dogs, psychological support dogs or mobility assist dogs.

Then, it was as if the blinking light changed to saying, "Mobility assist dog! Mobility assist dog! Mobility assist dog!" I thought, *What if this was something I could do for Chuck?*

I desperately wanted to do *something*. I don't have special medical or healing skills, so I couldn't help there. I don't have much money, so I couldn't offer to help financially, and I know he would have refused even if I had been able to do so. What I did have was a little black puppy dog named Boo, who might be an ideal service dog, with the right training, for someone who needed help around the house and some companionship. I knew from investigations how long the typical waiting list was for a service dog from a traditional service dog organization. I also knew that most organizations don't assign service dogs to people with a fatal diagnosis like ALS. A client of mine whose husband had ALS had been turned down by every service dog agency she contacted. Instead, she got a

German shepherd puppy and was hoping we could train the dog to be a companion for her husband. It was clear when I worked with her and her family just how much her husband enjoyed having the dog around. He told me one day that the dog would snuggle up between his legs as he sat in his wheelchair and just lean against him. He was thrilled with even this bit of companionship. I could only imagine how much Chuck would enjoy something like that— and perhaps a Little Boy Boo who could do even more.

I remembered Chuck's joy at meeting Atticus many Christmases earlier when I took him with me back to Lombard. I worried about taking Atticus in cargo and created quite a stir on the flight as I asked every flight attendant in the plane if they could check on my dog until the heavens seemed to speak to me, "TO THE WOMAN WHO KEEPS ASKING ABOUT HER DAWG—" of course, it was just the captain over the loudspeaker "—THE DAWG IS ABOARD." But all my anxiety and the effort of transporting Atticus were worth it. When I watched Chuck play with Atticus, I saw his eyes sparkle and his features soften like he was a kid again. On that trip, Atticus slept at the foot of my old bed with me in the house that had seen such abuse. It was the first time that I was ever able to sleep in that bed in peace. Maybe Boo could help Chuck feel more at ease with what he was going through now.

I knew it would be a lot of work to train Boo as a service dog because of the varied social skills he would need and the specific tasks he'd have to learn. I also knew that maybe sending Boo to another home would ultimately be the right thing for him. Since Lawrence wasn't warming up to him particularly quickly, I wondered if this was the reason Boo came to me: so I could give him to Chuck.

A mobility assist dog falls into the official category of "Service Dog" as defined by the Americans with Disabilities Act of 1990. A service dog is any dog who has been explicitly trained to perform a specific task or tasks for a person with a disability. Subsequent legislation has changed this definition slightly, but this is still the best basic description of a service dog. A mobility assist dog can pick things up for someone who has dropped something out of reach; turn on lights; get things from the refrigerator, a cabinet or a drawer; help with dressing and undressing; help a person stand up or move from wheelchair to bed or toilet; answer the door; fetch the phone; press a button on a special phone to call for help; or alert a family member of trouble—yes, just like Lassie telling everyone Timmy fell down a well. A mobility assist dog's services are limited only by the needs of the person and the aptitude of the dog.

Boo doesn't have to be able to do everything, I thought. *If he can pick up a few things, retrieve a few things and just be a companion, that will be enough.*

There was also a chance that Chuck and his family would say no to the gift. To take care of a dog costs money, and this was eventually going to be a one-income household with a young child to support and put through college. Chuck's wife might not want a dog around their cats, or my niece might be allergic. There were a lot of reasons they might not want this dog, no matter how well trained. I might not even be able to train Boo for the work. No matter how I looked at the situation, it was a long shot in the dark, but it was the only shot I had to help the only living relative who had supported me through some of the hardest times of my life.

Gram had been there for me, but she was long gone, and I never had the chance to thank her or repay her. I didn't want that to happen with Chuck.

So, I set about getting Boo ready without telling Chuck and his family. If I failed to train Boo to the tasks, Chuck wouldn't be disappointed, and if I presented Boo fully trained, Chuck was more likely to accept the gift. Armed with desperation and inherited pigheadedness, I began to consider the four levels of training that Boo would need to go through.

First, he would need to be introduced to a variety of places, people, sounds and smells, as well as anything else that he might encounter when working. We humans take for granted the environment we move through on a daily basis, not realizing that dogs can experience everyday things very differently than we do. The sound of the produce display units in the grocery store, for example, when they suddenly turn on to water the vegetables, can be pretty scary to a dog. Automatic doors that open with a *swoosh* can be startling and trigger movement responses. Revolving doors don't usually make much noise and are often pretty slow moving, but to many dogs, they just don't make sense—and dogs, like people, often shy away from things that don't make sense. Elevators are metal boxes with moving doors that apparently fly through the air without explanation. Even different floor surfaces can be creepy to walk on for some dogs. Tile, wood, linoleum, odd grates, stairs with and without risers and made with different surfaces—a working service dog has to be happy with encountering oddities like this at any time. I have had dogs in class who simply will not walk on the linoleum of the training space, and some dogs who have no problem with the linoleum absolutely refuse to enter the spooky hallway to the bathroom area because the floor is lit differently in there. Boo would have to be ready for any of these situations in order to help Chuck.

Second, Boo needed skills—the standard foundation skills that from my perspective as a trainer, all dogs need: sit, down, stay, settle, wait, leave it, drop it, say hello (only when asked) and walk nicely on a leash with a person (in Boo's case, potentially a person with an unsteady gait or using a wheelchair). Service dogs have to be able to perform these skills in highly distracting environments: sit and stay in an elevator, walk politely through a revolving door that's coming around to get them from the backside, sit and stay while the produce case in the grocery store makes funny noises and sprays water everywhere, wait patiently while the security check point person searches the handler, wait outside an elevator (holding place as the doors open with a ding or beep, and people rush out) and have no reactions to overhead PA announcements or the bustling of a crowded airport or train station. Service dogs also need to settle under tables in busy restaurants, with yummy-smelling food going by—maybe even food on the floor right in front of their noses—so a solid leave it is necessary. Take it and drop it commands are high on the list for mobility assist dogs because they're expected to pick up and deliver items to their humans.

For many service dogs, greeting people can be the hardest skill to master. We want service dogs to be social, and social dogs want to say hello, but when they are working, they can't say hello unless the handler gives them permission with a command. Imagine what would happen to an individual with a visual disability whose guide dog decided to go say hello to a smiling stranger instead of stopping the handler from entering a crosswalk against the light? This is tough when a stranger is smiling at the dog, giving the dog all the human body language cues that say, "I'm friendly, and I know just where to scratch your ear." The dog has to ignore all that unless he is given the command to say hello.

Last, Boo would have to master specific tasks that he would need to perform for Chuck, like picking up dropped items and bringing them to Chuck, or retrieving designated items—a bottle of medicine, a blanket—or whatever else Chuck might need. Boo was never going to grow big enough to be a brace dog for a six-foot-two man (a brace dog can help a person into or out of a wheelchair, help someone move from a seated position to a standing position and even sometimes help balance them when standing and walking, so naturally, these dogs need to meet size criteria), but Boo might be asked to wear a backpack and carry items Chuck could not. Boo would have to learn to ride in a car in the typical service dog position, on the floor between Chuck's feet. Boo would also need to learn how to open cabinets, drawers and even doors using a special device on the handle. He would need to be able to alert other family members if there was a problem and retrieve a special phone, like the K-9 Rescue Phone, and bring it to Chuck or hit the button on the phone in an emergency. (The K-9 Rescue Phone has a dog-proof plate over the dialing buttons so dogs don't inadvertently dial the phone when carrying it to their handlers. Just above that protective plate, it has a two-and-a-half-inch white button that gives the dog a large, easily visible, high-contrast target in case he has to make the emergency call. The dogs can be taught to depress this large button by pawing or with a nose nudge if their humans are seizing, having a heart attack, having trouble breathing or unresponsive.) Boo would also need to be able to snuggle up for petting and just be there for loving when Chuck was alone during the day when he was no longer working.

One of the bigger hurdles for Boo would be to follow computer commands. Because of the nature of Chuck's ALS and the early loss of his speech, he started using a computer to communicate long before he was immobile. Boo would have to be able to comply with commands that Chuck would enter into his keyboard. It was going to be cumbersome and frustratingly slow for Chuck—the quick-witted man who always knew the answers to *Jeopardy!* before anyone else—and it meant that Boo would have to follow commands from a disembodied computer voice, either word commands or tones that signaled certain behaviors. Most dogs are usually being cued by our body language in addition to our words, but Boo would only be able to rely on the computer words or tones. Once Boo was trained for the tasks using traditional commands, we would transfer those onto a secondary command that we would already have worked out on the computer. Computer macros could be written so Chuck could tap just two keys on the keyboard to say "get phone" or "pick up paper" and so on. Luckily for us, teaching dogs second commands for a behavior they already know often produces a more reliable command.

Boo had no idea what I was planning for him. At three months and still working on his potty-training in the middle of that hard, horrible winter, he was going to embark on one of the greatest journeys any dog can take. Planning for Boo's training, I considered his age because age plays a role in the design of different social-ization and training programs. It struck me that since his litter was about five or six weeks old on Halloween, that would put little baby Boo's birthday just a week after Chuck's in September. A happy coincidence—perhaps even a good omen.

5

The Class Dunce

I had trained hundreds of pet dogs,
dozens of visiting therapeutic activities dogs and
even some companion dogs for people with disabilities. Although part of me always expects—
and fears—the worst, I felt fairly confident,
given my successes up to this point, that I would
be able to get Boo up to speed to be a service
dog for Chuck. After all, if I could train Dante,
the flying-through-the-air street dog from
Brooklyn, to walk politely on leash and greet
people calmly but enthusiastically, how difficult
could it be for me to teach Boo to pick up a few
things on command, open a couple cabinets and
drawers and just be there for Chuck?

The first step would have to be socialization.

Standard pet-dog puppy classes, like the ones I
was teaching, are usually about three things:
socializing, basic skills and owner awareness.
Fun for all, with puppies madly dashing back and
forth, skidding across the floor because their feet
and legs aren't yet fitted to their brains (and
sometimes vice versa), these classes can look
like nothing but madcap puppy mayhem. In fact,
amid all that flying fur, puppies are being
socialized with other dogs their age to develop

and eventually maintain good dog social skills. Sometimes they are called away from their puppy pratfalls to work on basic skills like sit, down, stay or politely greeting humans and dogs; then, when they return to their puppy play— grabbing, biting, holding, pouncing, chasing and more—their handlers are learning about appropriate versus inappropriate play, how to encourage the former and what to do about the latter. Some classes are arranged so dogs spend most of their time playing with each other, with a few commands in the mix; others weigh skills more heavily but make sure there's a good bit of open-play socialization as well. Although classes can have wildly different structures, the goals for all of them are the same: well-socialized, confident puppies who are ready to learn.

These types of puppy classes weren't enough for what I was hoping to do with Boo. He needed something more like the adult-dog classes I was teaching for H.A.R.T. Programs but geared toward puppies.

I was talking about my plans for Boo with one of my H.A.R.T. colleagues who assisted the local guide-dog puppy-training class, and she offered to sneak him into this class. It would be perfect for Boo's needs because it included skills and socialization but also aimed to make dogs comfortable around stressors and distractions they might meet while working: strange surfaces, surprising sounds, unusual people, you name it. If dogs have learned to stay cheerful and jolly when they run into something unexpected or even frightening, they'll be much more effective working dogs. It's only after going through basic training that all working dogs get their specialized training; therapy dogs learn general tasks for social visiting, for example, and service dogs learn specific tasks.

We had already begun working on sit, down, stay, wait, walk on leash and a few more commands. Boo was not the quickest learner in the potty-training arena, which was still a work in progress, but he seemed to be catching on to the basics of sit, down and wait when we worked alone. If Dante or Atticus was around when we trained, though, it was as if I disappeared from Boo's view. At the end of January 2001, Boo seemed like a sensitive and social, albeit highly distracted, dog who just couldn't catch onto potty-training. I was excited to get Boo to start learning ways to help Chuck in a classroom situation, which would offer us the socialization and fundamental skills outside the home that Boo so needed.

Or it would have been, if I'd been able to get Boo to the class in a happy state of mind, ready for work, but he hated my truck. It was an older manual-transmission pickup. There was a mystery breeze in the cab when I went over forty miles per hour, and it made strange noises when I shifted gears. To be honest, I was shocked every time it squeaked past inspection. The only two riding options for Boo were the floor (closer to the strange noises, which he hated) or the seat next to me (closer to the mystery breeze, which he also hated). Either choice gave me a frightened little dog flopping around the truck, offering every terrified canine body language cue a dog could.

Each week as we ventured out to class, I was filled with hope: hope that this would be the week he loved the truck and loved the class, hope that he would learn quickly and happily as we built the skills he needed to help Chuck. And each week Boo paced, whined and flailed around the tiny cab for the entire forty-five-minute ride to puppy class. I sang to him (many dogs love music, and Boo is a big fan of ABBA; "Water-Boo" is his favorite), I jollied him and I pleaded with him to magically calm down in hopes that he would understand the importance of his future work.

It was in the middle of one of my songs when I realized how life-threatening this class was going to be—for both of us. Navigating the truck onto a busy, four-lane highway always resulted in Boo climbing up my arm to the top of my head, trying any way he could to escape from the loud, scary, accelerating metal boxes that seemed to be closing in on the scary metal box in which he was already trapped. By the time we got to class, he was stressed beyond belief, as was I.

Stress and excitement combined to create the Boo tractor pull as we entered the training space that first day, and he plowed toward the other dogs in class who were working at military attention by comparison. Boo needed to communicate with the other puppies. Dogs still made more sense to him than some people. These puppies offered him something he understood in a new, confusing place.

"Boo, Boo, Boo!" I called in my no-fail, high-pitched Boo call. No response. At home, this would always get him to turn his head and come running, but not here. I did, however, manage to get the attention of every *other* dog and human in the class, leading some annoyed handlers to struggle to get their little-toy-soldier puppies back to sitting at attention while they tried to ignore the slapstick routine that Boo and I were rapidly becoming.

I tried again: "Boo, toy, play?" I squeaked, squeaked, squeaked the training toy I always had in my treat pouch. Nothing. Just tractor Boo toward the other dogs who were far more fascinating than I could ever be—and, of course, all once again looking at me, probably hoping they could have Boo's toy. Again I heard muffled, frustrated comments from the other handlers as they tried to get their puppies to ignore my antics.

I started making noises—horsey sounds, chicken sounds, sounds that I'm sure solidified the growing belief among the other people in the class that I was crazy. Oblivious to me, my silly Boo just kept vaulting in the direction of the nearest puppy. "I'm so sorry," I said to the other teams with a laugh that I hoped didn't sound as desperate as it felt. "He's just excited." As I spoke, the motion of Boo's vaulting jolted treats out of my hand and training pouch. Now every food-driven Lab in that room was as interested in Boo, or at least the treats scattered around him, as he was in them. Some of the teams tried to politely move away from the rabble-rouser, while others made no effort to disguise their disdain for me and my mutt.

As I continued to try to explain away my dog's behavior, Boo was shamelessly flirting with the other dogs by making every manner of monkey noise a dog could make. Vaulting wildly at the end of the tight leash, he was unable to relax or refocus on me. It was clear that he was starting to have trouble breathing because of the pressure on his throat, so I moved toward him by simply keeping the pressure on the leash and then moved closer to him without letting him pull forward. As soon as I was close enough, I slipped one hand under his collar, placed the other over his breastbone to relieve some of the pressure on his throat, and once he was no longer pulling, I squished his butt into a sit. He was still making his bizarre monkey noises, but at least he was stationary. I don't like to squish a dog into a sit and never advise clients to do so (forcing a dog into a sit does not teach the dog a reliable, confident sit; it teaches the dog that you are forceful and that he has two choices: comply with your force or fight back), but I figured that if I didn't contain him soon, we'd be tossed out of class.

All my hope and excitement was smashed in the ninety seconds it took for us to walk in, disrupt everything and everyone and squish Boo into a sit.

By the end of that disastrous first class, other students suggested I try different training treats, and for our times in the truck, try tying the leash to the seat to keep him from flopping all over. I did that for the ride home, but he simply pulled furiously on the leash as he desperately tried to get to me for support. This engaged his oppositional reflex (which I didn't know at the time) and only served to increase his stress and anxiety. Although he didn't end up on my head, he was exhausted, panting heavily and still managed to climb up as far as he could to get next to me while still being tied to the seat. We didn't try that again.

• • •

The evening of the second class, I anxiously wondered what could make Boo happy in the truck and what on Earth might make him focus in class. I had experimented with various treats during the intervening week. I found some that could even make him focus on me while working around Dante and Atticus, and I was sure these would work in class and maybe even in the truck.

No luck in the truck. He was still not taking even the puppy-crack treats I had concocted out of several different stinky treats. I tried more songs like Lawrence's "Crazy Li'l Pup," which usually calmed Boo at home. I was shifting, merging, flinging treats and singing, "Crazy li'l pup named Booooo likes to go pee and pooooo; any 'ol place will doooo . . . ," yet Boo still climbed on my head as we pulled onto the highway, leaving treats scattered all over the floor of the truck.

Standing outside the church where the classes were held, I felt for my treat pouch like a soldier feeling for her weapon and hoped the empty hope of the damned as I watched all the toy-soldier pups focused on their handlers for plain old dog food as they readied to enter class. Knowing that I had to find something that would interest Boo during class, I experimented with various treats to see what would make him vibrate with joy. In addition to the puppy-crack-treat concoction that made Lawrence gag just to smell it, I found that radishes made Boo come running from anywhere in the house.

But once Boo saw the other dogs in class, the radishes, the puppy crack and I were unimportant to him again. The other, usually focused puppies tried to ignore him, but since I had seriously upped the stink factor with my puppy crack, every Lab in the room was focused on my treat pouch. All the other handlers either thought I was nuts for bringing radishes, pissed off at me for bringing the puppy crack that distracted their dogs or annoyed at Boo for creating a ruckus. Why we weren't drummed out of class at that moment, I don't know. It was clear that Boo and I did not belong.

The other puppies in the class were bred specifically from chosen lines of working dogs. Before entering this phase of their training, they had all been tested several times for temperament and intelligence. The result was that the class was composed of (1) the best, the brightest, the smartest, the most focused and the most stable dogs, and (2) Boo. In class, all those commands I'd gotten him to do at home were clearly just whispers on a faraway breeze that he could barely hear. The only thing he was able to focus on was trying to romp with the other dogs, which made him apparently unable to see, or hear, anything else. And when I attempted to stop him physically with the leash or by squishing him into a sit, he simply melted down and tried to become invisible.

Now, I know that a lack of focus and an inability to take treats are both indicators of a dog stressed over his threshold. Low levels of stress can actually facilitate learning, but we have to be very careful, as the neurological learning processes encouraged and supported by low levels of stress can be hindered or completely halted by higher levels of stress. Training is best when it is an emotionally enjoyable activity that builds a solid relationship between dog and handler while bathing the dog's brain in the ideal neurotransmitters and hormones for learning. I just couldn't find Boo's place of low-level stress.

Boo, like most of the other dogs in the class, was around four and a half months old, but a simple comparison by age was deceiving. The organization that bred the other dogs in the class had planned this training from the time the dogs were born. Their puppies had received the neurological stimulation and exposure to new places, people, sounds, sights and smells that are vital in the early weeks for building an engaged dog capable of full physical, emotional and behavioral health. The early three-to-sixteen-day phase is critical for neurological stimulation (the Bio-Sensor Program developed by the U.S.

military to build a better dog is used during this time). Without good neurological stimulation in those early days, puppies can grow up with physical, emotional and behavioral deficits. For puppies to grow into dogs who are unafraid of new and strange people, things and environments when they grow older, they must be happily exposed to a wide variety of novel stimuli through the end of the socialization window and beyond. Further socialization continues until the dogs are adults in order to preserve all the good work done early on.

I have no idea what neurological stimulation and exposure Boo received in his early weeks, but given that he'd been left on the stoop of a strip-mall pet store in a box, I'm willing to bet the answer is not much. For the first few weeks after we brought him home, he dreamed of nursing and suckling (it's a heartbreaking sight to watch a lonely little puppy suckle an imaginary nipple in his sleep). It was clear that Boo had not had the early advantages the other puppies in this class had. We were waging an uphill battle.

Regarding his truck issues, I was told unequivocally *not* to soothe him or talk to him in the truck. "You have to stop comforting him, Lisa," said the assistant, unsuccessfully concealing her irritation at Boo (and me). "When you soothe him or sing to him, whatever, it only rewards his bad behavior. You are only reinforcing his fears and making him more fearful. The way to get him to fall in line is to show him that acting out isn't going to get him anything from you."

Hindsight is a blessing and a curse. It would require a whole other book to detail just how wrong and ultimately how harmful the phrase "you are only reinforcing his fears" was. Fears and emotions are very complicated and require more than just being ignored to be remedied. This truck phobia was my first lesson in what overstressing can do to a dog.

I understood overstressing from my own experience. After my near-drowning episode, I was terrified of water, but this didn't stop my father from trying desperately to get me back into the pool. I remember standing defiantly on the edge of the pool (some would say dominantly), refusing to enter the terrible water. Dad eventually pulled me in and held me afloat in the water, hoping I would see that the water wasn't something to fear.

All our brains are equipped with survival instincts in the limbic system. It's possible to learn after only one experience that a situation is life-threatening; subsequently, that situation can become an instant, automatic fear-response trigger. That old part of the brain is hardwired for survival and will dig in against whatever nonsense it thinks the newer part of the brain is trying to sell it. If we want to change that fear, the procedure of desensitizing and counter-conditioning is a long and slow process.

While my father was trying very hard to help, he was also impatient. Ironically, he only further solidified my fear of water through the act of flooding (pushing someone into an experience they fear and hoping the individual will see that what they fear will not kill them)—but flooding can backfire, as it did with me. This experience has given me a strong sense of empathy when I'm working with fearful dogs. Because I've been there, I know how important it is to be patient and go at the animal's pace. Had I not learned these lessons and adapted them for Boo, his story would have turned out very differently.

I hoped every class would be better than the last, but once overstressed by the truck ride, all Boo could do was bounce around the training room. The class became a canine pinball game with Boo setting off all the other puppies by making monkey noises at them or panting his crazy happy pant right in their faces. When all hope was lost, I would throw off any notions of shame and begin to make quick bubble noises in high-pitched tones. At home, those bubble noises got all three dogs' attention every time, but in class, of course, it got every other dog's attention except mine. Each week, I was just a tiny voice in the wilderness of his brain. Boo was like an unruly, undisciplined kid dropped all of a sudden into the middle of AP Chemistry. He paid no attention to the teacher, only wanted to talk to his friends and didn't understand why nobody else was dying to turn the Bunsen burner up as high as it would go and see what happened.

Boo and I were the class losers, like Spicoli from *Fast Times at Ridgemont High*, always causing distractions and disruptions and never seeming to learn anything. Sometimes Boo just looked stoned, staring into space indiscriminately. All week long between classes, I practiced with him at home. He would sit, stay, down, walk nicely, leave it, and do everything I asked of him. Then, we would get into the scary truck and go to class, where he would either whine and whirl at the end of his leash in some weird Boo form of flirting with the other dogs or, worse, just stare up into the air at nothing. The class teacher—and all the other students in the class—assumed I was a bad trainer of a bad dog.

All the confidence I built while training Dante, other H.A.R.T. dogs and the dogs I taught in my classes and consultations washed away each week in Boo's class, yet I persisted. I had a dream for this little dog. Class after class, I brought new puppy-crack recipes that Boo flipped over while training during the week at home. Once the other handlers realized that Boo and I weren't vacating the class, they learned to roll with my unusual approach to Boo, and my treat experiments became a running joke. Each week the other handlers watched as Boo refused another super-special, high-value treat that their dogs would have killed for. I danced for him, sang for him and made strange, silly, embarrassing noises for him. I trotted out every treat known to excite dogkind, and still Boo wouldn't pay one nanosecond of attention to me. No one knew what to do.

Now I look back and know that Boo should not have been in that class. He made progress, but it was just hard to measure vis-à-vis the über-puppies alongside him. By the end of the fifth or sixth class, his distractions were intermittently interruptible, and he actually paid some attention to me occasionally. I know now that I should have gone more slowly with him, but no one suggested that at the time. Instead, they advised, "Don't let him get away with it." I bristled, remembering the "work" I did with Dad after the near-drowning episode. I hadn't been trying to get away with anything by not going into that water; I had been terrified. When I tried to explain that Boo was probably overwhelmed and stressed, I was advised to do collar corrections, also known as pop-and-jerk training. It seemed cruel to me, but this teacher was the expert, so I gave it a try. Boo's only reaction was to look even more stoned, be even less responsive and do that Boo "I'm invisible" thing.

Meanwhile, I was more and more physically exhausted. Although I only made the commute to Manhattan two or three days a week, that was enough to feed my chronic joint pains, especially in my knees. The pain and swelling in my knees eventually forced me to sit on the floor during puppy class, at which point Boo was no longer the only one in trouble. I was quietly but sternly forbidden to sit during the lecture portion.

I didn't know how to explain the excruciating pain I felt when I stood for the entire lecture. My pain was finally manageable, thanks to a wonderful homeopath and a couple of great acupuncturists, who gave me back a big chunk of my life and reduced my pain to something I could live with. Yet, there were still times like these, standing at the end of a long day, when it could be excruciating. Although using a cane gave me relief and support without the medical side effects of the typical lupus cocktail of prednisone and plaquenil, training a dog with a cane proved to be very cumbersome. And with or without a cane, holding a leash with a dog at the end of it who twists and flies through the air torques the knee joints with each spin and whirl the dog makes. The pain I felt wasn't com-pletely for naught—at least I learned that an uncomfortable handler makes for an uncomfortable dog. Whenever I teach now, I make sure there are chairs for folks who need them.

The irony was that when I was moving and training Boo, I could work through the pain. It was only when I had to stand still for the lecture portions of the class that it all came throbbing back. I've come to realize that this is an important feature of animal-assisted therapeutic activities: people will frequently do things they truly enjoy despite feeling pain because when we're engaged in activities we love, the brain fires differently and produces different happy-making neurochemicals than at other times.

To put it another way, my first experience with animal-assisted rehabilitation occurred when I accidentally rehabilitated myself.

Despite the benefits, it became clear that Boo and I had outstayed our welcome in guide-puppy training, so we regretfully bid the class farewell. But I wasn't going to give up on the idea of training Boo to help my brother, so I decided to find another class for him to take, maybe one that was more basic.

First, though, I had to get him into the truck without freaking out so he would be receptive to training when he got to class. As an official service dog for Chuck, he'd have to be comfortable riding at Chuck's feet in a car, so this was essential training anyway. All three dogs always became very excited and ran out to meet me when I came home from work, and it occurred to me that we might be able to use this to train Boo.

Making an association between a scary thing and a really, really fun thing is extremely useful in training. This is just what Chuck did, without even knowing what he was doing at the time, when he started the process of desensitizing me to scary water. By taking me to the pool with him time and time again, never pushing me to go in farther than I could handle and always taking a break from frolicking in the deep end to check up on me floundering in the shallow end, he let me make the association that if I went to the scary pool, I got to have fun time with my brother.

My plan for Boo was simple: if he could approach the scary truck, he would get to have me all to himself for his greeting, and the happy association would begin. I ran the plan by Lawrence, and he laughed and said, "That might be just the thing the little monkey dog needs." If Lawrence was coming up with nicknames for Boo, I knew he was warming up to the little guy—even if he couldn't admit it.

I parked the truck in the driveway, shut off the engine and didn't get out. All three dogs were barking, including Boo with his usual howl-like "Whoo, whoo, whoo." Lawrence let Boo out alone, and he ran toward me but stopped short when he realized that I was still in the monster box. I understood his dilemma: to greet me, he would have to put his paws inside the scary truck. After a few moments during which I could see the puzzle work itself out on his face, he finally came up cautiously and gingerly put his paws inside. I gave him treat after treat along with some primo butt scratching.

Because Boo is always thrilled to see me come home, this began to shape a really positive association for him with the truck. It was turning into the wonderful metal box that brought me home. This was classical conditioning way outside the box, but I suspect that even Drs. Pavlov and Premack would have nodded in approval at the use of me as the primary reinforcer to begin the process of desensitizing and counterconditioning Boo's fear of the truck.

In about a month, Boo went from jumping into the truck to greet me for play and treats to being content to ride up and down the driveway while still remaining happy and taking treats. *Yeah!* This was how to expose a dog to a new scary stimulus while keeping him subthreshold. I was getting a handle on this!

I enrolled Boo in a basic class taught by another trainer at the store where I taught. We lasted a whole two weeks in that one. Boo was still the panting, frenzied lunatic at the end of the leash trying to engage any dog in play, but at least he wasn't stressed by the truck anymore. The space for the class was small, and the dogs were effectively on top of one another. Every dog in this class was distracted out of their minds, not just Boo. An overstressed Australian cattle dog classmate took a marked dislike to Boo, lunging and snapping at him in a way that terrified not just Boo but me too.

The politics of the situation made it tough for me to ask the trainer to do something about the dog behaving aggressively. Fearing that Boo might lose his good social skills and develop a fear of other dogs if the Australian cattle dog kept threatening him every week, I decided to stop going to this class. If I wanted to train Boo, I realized, I had to do it myself.

I started to let Boo hang out in a crate during the classes I taught, then work with him in the store after and in between sessions. The main problem was still that he wasn't taking treats outside of the house, except for in the driveway. His attention was sporadic, and when I did have it, my praise was fundamentally meaningless because he wouldn't take the treat.

Trainers have two ways of getting a dog's focus: something rewarding like food or toys to lure and shape attention or something punishing like a yank on the leash (or worse) when the dog doesn't pay attention. I kept hearing all the voices of traditional trainers saying, "You just have to be firm and show him who's boss," so I bought a plastic pinch collar for Boo. The only time I used it, Boo didn't pay attention, and he actually moved farther away and went into Boo World, where he shuts down and hopes to be invisible—just like my own shutdown responses to so many childhood events. When I thought of it like that, I could only conclude that I was obligated to find better options for training than pain and fear. The scientific evidence shows clearly what works and why and predicts the fallout of punishment, from behavior like Boo's minor shutdown to the more severe, aggressive responses. I gladly went back to positive reinforcement only and worked very slowly and patiently to build his confidence, skills and treat-taking capacities in ever increasingly distracting environments.

Boo's pace was incredibly frustrating, especially as Chuck's ALS was progressing quickly, and I didn't want to think I might not be able to get Boo to my brother in time for him to be helpful. In e-mails and conversations, everybody held firm to the Edwards rules of engagement: no revealing feelings, personal information or other tawdry details of our lives. There was never any specific mention of the progression of the disease, only references to new limitations that Chuck had: the complete need for a computer to facilitate speaking, a ramp for a wheelchair and the mention that his ability to continue working was coming to an end. Between what was said and what wasn't, it was easy, and heartbreaking, to see how rapidly the disease was progressing.

The one positive thing we had going for us at this point in Boo's training was that humans now made sense to Boo. He started to love going out to see people on our training and socializing adventures. I just needed to find a reinforcer that he would respond to away from home. One day I wondered, *Well, he's an outside-the-box dog, so why am I using treats from inside a box?* I put an inside-out, zip-top baggie over my hand, reached into a jar of peanut butter, grabbed a big handful and turned the bag right-side out again. Later, when we visited a pet store and I asked him to sit, holding the delicious peanut butter puppet right in front of his nose, he sat! When I rewarded him with the peanut butter, the scent was his first treat; then he got some on his nose, which meant he could enjoy it a second time by licking it off. He repeated the sit, and I knew I had found Boo's reward.

The magic of super-stinky puppet reinforcers like peanut butter (or if you're allergic to peanuts, cream cheese or liverwurst) has to do with the activity in a dog's brain while he sniffs. Dogs have as many as two hundred and fifty million olfactory receptors in their nasal cavities, compared with humans who have only five to forty million. Because so much of the dog's brain is involved in processing scents, from the forebrain way back to the limbic system (stopping for a chat in between with our friend the amygdala, the "holy crap" center of the brain), stronger scents can jolt a dog out of a distracted state and get him to focus when not much else can. It's as if the door to the dog's thinking brain were being held shut by emotion. Super-stinky reinforcers make the emotion ease up just enough for us to get the door to the thinking brain open just a little. It's as if the dog's brain says, "*There's something I have to bark at! I absolutely must bark right n*—oooh, peanut butter? That looks interesting. Maybe I should have a look. Wait, was I about to start barking at something? I can get to that later. There's peanut butter here now. Peanut butter, yum. Did you say sit? Of course I'll sit. After all, there's peanut butter here!"

The peanut butter puppets worked well, but they weren't magic. Boo's skills were still unreliable at times, especially in basics like potty-training. He'd go for days without making any mistakes, and then we'd have a week of missed pees and poops. Getting him out at the right time wasn't working as a strategy because there was no right time—he didn't have a pattern to his eliminations. So I started taking him out every time he blinked. Lawrence complained that Boo wouldn't learn to hold it if I trained him that way, and I countered that I couldn't crate him hours and hours every day because he had shown an inability to hold it. He would just learn to pee in the crate. Often I'd take Boo out because he looked like he really needed to poop, and he'd become mesmerized by something in the wind or a sound far away and forget what he was doing—just staring into nowhere. In the end, potty-training for Boo took a year.

Although I was starting to feel discouraged, I continued to work on the other skills that Boo would need in order to be valuable to Chuck. The retrieve command is a chained command, which means that it's made up of several foundation commands, in this case, go out, pick it up, carry it and drop it. Boo was terrific at drop it but not so good at pick it up. His best drop it came one day when he trotted quickly past me with his head down—the signal that he had something in his mouth he didn't want to lose. "Drop it," I said suspiciously, and out of his mouth came the pincushion filled with pins and needles. He received the greatest series of "good boys" in the world for that as I ran to get him some treats for his big reward.

After you have chained a good retrieve, you teach dogs the names of various objects that they'll need to bring to their handlers. Boo still didn't know pick it up or carry it, so I couldn't start teaching him names yet—he was already dazed and confused just by the retrieve chain. We worked on the tug command, too—necessary for dogs who might be asked to open a door or cabinet outfitted with a special tugging attachment, and used to help people dress or undress—but Boo could never tug anything but my socks. He would pull my sock off and drop it for me on command. Then, I would put the sock back on, and we would start all over again. But when it came to anything I wasn't wearing on my foot, he couldn't seem to stabilize himself against the pressure coming from the other end of the tug item. I hoped this was something that would right itself with his physical development, but it wasn't changing. He couldn't tug, he couldn't pick things up, he couldn't save his business reliably for outdoors—we were stuck in a quagmire, and I was more and more frustrated.

Answers came one day when Boo, Dante and I were out walking with two veterinarians from the animal hospital, Cindy and Julie. Dante divided his time on this walk between his usual laser-like focus on me and flirting with Cindy's two black Labs and Julie's golden retriever. (It was Cindy's Lab Olympia who inspired Dante to hump at age five. He never lost his interest in her, which made for difficult questions later when they would visit classrooms together. We strategically planned to be sure Dante was never *behind* her.)

As we walked, Boo continuously wandered aimlessly away from us all, bumping into logs and tree stumps as if he weren't looking or couldn't see where he was going, not checking back to keep an eye on me. When I called him, he just looked around with a bewildered expression, seemingly not able to tell where I was. Each time he wandered away, I had to retrieve him and escort him back to the group. All the way back, he would trot his usual show pony trot that had his half-bent ears flapping like a bird's wings. During the hour in which we made our way around the beautiful and bucolic North Salem Open Land Foundation, Boo wandered off probably a dozen times—sometimes within seconds of rejoining the group. In between episodes of wandering off, he would stop and look up at nothing.

After awhile, Julie started watching him more closely. She asked if he always walked with the funny gait that made him look like a trotting show pony, which she said actually had a medical name, dysmetric gait.

"Yes," I said. "It's his silly puppy-walking."

She asked about his confusion, the wandering, his staring at nothing.

"That's Boo."

She suggested to Cindy that Boo might have a

138

syndrome called cerebellar hypoplasia. "What do you think?" she asked. I watched the two very empirically oriented women cycle through everything in their heads.

Cindy nodded. "It makes sense."

"Cerebellar hypoplasia?" I asked tentatively.

Cerebellar hypoplasia, they explained to me, is the name for a condition that occurs in utero and results in a cerebellum (part of the brain) that is not completely mature at birth. In humans, the symptoms of cerebellar hypoplasia can include delayed development, mental retardation, ataxia (poor balance), seizures, hearing impairment, reduced muscle tone and more. Symptoms in dogs, although not exactly the same, can be very similar.

This condition, they said, could account for Boo's lack of normal progress in training; his unusual, high-stepping, clumsy gait; light-headedness; and poor concentration. It appeared that his vision issues were neurological, but he may well have had other acuity issues, too. Because difficulty with movement and tremors are a part of cerebellar hypoplasia, it made sense that Boo just froze sometimes—he was probably trying to stabilize himself. It was clear that the one-year-old Boo had been struggling much more than I realized.

As Julie and Cindy explained this disorder, my jaw dropped as my heart struggled to comprehend the conflicting implications of what I was learning. On the one hand, I had a reason for Boo's slow progress other than that I was a crappy trainer. In fact, it was probably just the opposite: I had managed to train, albeit slowly and only moderately, a dog with developmental disabilities. I had to give Boo credit for trying to keep up with everything I asked of him in spite of how hard it must have been. I was indescribably proud of Boo's efforts.

On the other hand, I had to face reality. This little dog would never be able to learn what he needed to in order to be the service dog I wanted him to be for Chuck.

But I realized, too, that Boo and I had some things in common, and maybe he was here to help me patch up some of my old emotional potholes. It was like a cliché scene from an old movie when the foggy filter slowly crossed the screen, and you know you're now in a flashback. Julie and Cindy's explanation of cerebellar hypoplasia brought back Dr. Maglione's voice explaining that I couldn't read because I was dyslexic, that I had a pretty good IQ, but it was hobbled by the dyslexia. I had wanted so badly to be smart, and I knew Boo wanted so badly to do what I was asking, but neither one of us could be what we wanted to be.

Then, as in all clichéd flashbacks, I heard a small voice in my head trying desperately to cut through the pity I was stuck in for myself and Boo. I remembered that of the many tests Dr. Maglione gave me over our weeks of working together, there was one in which, while I just thought it was fun, I astonished him with what he called my brilliance. At the end of a test that involved putting differently shaped wood pieces into their respective holes—three times: once with my eyes open using my dominant hand, once blindfolded using my dominant hand and lastly blindfolded using my nondominant hand—he told me I scored higher than anyone he had ever tested. He marveled at that skill and was very eager to share my test scores with his colleagues. Neither one of us knew what to do with them, but I had a skill! In later years, when I got a car, I realized how useful that skill was: no one can pack a trunk as fully and precisely as I can. But more seriously, it was this skill at finding and remembering micropatterns that has given me gifts beyond measure when training dogs.

If I had a skill, then there had to be something Boo could do, and I just needed to find it. Boo's special needs were not going to be ignored or hidden. He would be who he was, and he would get whatever help I could give him to make him the best he could be with what he had. How it made me look as a trainer was unimportant. Let the silly attention-getting noises continue!

I thought for a brief moment that maybe Boo could be a companion for Chuck—not a service dog but just good company—but that would still take a good deal of training, and the truth was that Chuck's family didn't need a dog with special needs at a time when Chuck was getting sicker by the day. Boo would have been a burden for them—a cuddly, loving, super-soft burden, to be sure, but a burden nonetheless. Despite my newfound pride in Boo, my heart was broken and deflated.

Shortly after I told Lawrence about Julie and Cindy's diagnosis, I could see him having a change of heart toward the little guy. Maybe learning that Boo had cerebellar hypoplasia helped Lawrence understand that Boo's slow response to training wasn't something he was doing on purpose, just to be ornery. It was simply a function of the way his little puppy brain allowed him to learn things.

I first noticed Lawrence's changing attitude when I came home from class one night to find him zooming around the house with Boo balanced on his hands, chasing Dante and Atticus from room to room while making little-boy airplane noises. "You're not having fun playing with Boo, are you?!"

"I am *not playing* with Boo," he insisted. "I am using Boo as a *fighter plane* to chase *Dante and Atticus*."

"Oh," I said, suppressing a smile. "I should have known."

I was happy with the small miracles.

We got Boo on Halloween of 2000, and September 2001 looked like it was going to be Chuck's last birthday. I now knew that there was nothing I could give him at this point except my correspondence and holiday visits. Through our e-mails, we revisited our love of movies, and I turned him onto *Babylon 5*, a sci-fi series. Both Chuck and I loved science fiction—he was a science guy and a literary guy. *Babylon 5* harked back to the old movies we used to watch—it was a World War II movie in a science fiction setting. It didn't get more perfect for us.

When I went to Chuck's house in Lombard for what was to be my last Christmas visit, I brought along some *Babylon 5* movies on DVD. Normally, Chuck's wife and daughter wouldn't be caught anywhere near a show like that, but perhaps they sensed that they wouldn't have another opportunity to participate in the venerable Chuck/ Lisa B-movie tradition, so we all watched together. If it was possible to find joy in any of this, there were a few moments. When we cannot speak, we manage to communicate in other ways. Chuck's eyes told the whole story when he looked at his wife and daughter. His love and longing for them filled the silence and the space between them where there could no longer be words.

Chuck's wife mentioned to me during my visit that their cats played a great role in helping him through the days when he was home alone. Although they couldn't pick things up or open cabinets for him, one of the cats would sit on the arm of his chair for hours snuggled up against him, and when Chuck could no longer reach out to pet them, the other cat actually taught herself to burrow her way under his arm. She would do this over and over again, as if she were doing the petting for both of them. It was bittersweet. I was disappointed that I was not able to give him Boo—even if only for a little help and comfort near the end—but I was happy that Chuck had the animal companionship that I knew he craved.

6
Canine Assistance
Post-9/11

On the second Tuesday of Boo's first September, Mom and Dad were flying to Chicago from Florida to see Chuck for what they believed was probably going to be one of his last birthdays, on the 13th. (Halloween will always, for me, be associated with bringing Boo home, and September 13 will always be my brother's birthday.) I was working from home, awaiting the arrival of the bug man. The autumn always called for a full spray of the outside of the house for spiders, ants and other opportunistic critters that might try to move into our warm home as the outside temperatures began to drop.

Boo was closing in on his first full year on this planet. His service-dog training for Chuck had come to a grinding halt, and his potty-training was still stalled at unreliable, with intermittent successes, but at least now I had a reason.

When the bug man showed up, I put down my coffee and took advantage of his arrival for puppy socialization exercises. As the morning news played in the background, I asked him to pet the dogs, especially the puppy in training (no matter what Boo did with his life, he still needed to be a social dog). The bug man was happy to comply and pet the dogs before descending into the dark and icky crawl space. Nothing could have been more mundane that second Tuesday in Boo's first September than the scene of the bug man and me standing in my kitchen, reviewing the disclaimer for the toxins he was going to be spraying on the outside of the house.

"You know this one. We used it last time," he said. "It'll take about two hours to dry, so keep the dogs inside until then."

"Will do," I said, as I signed the form.

"And this paper is just to remind you to keep the pets away from the bait. I always put it where they can't get it, but—"

"This just in," said the anchor on the TV. "You are looking at obviously a very disturbing, live shot. That is the World Trade Center there, and we have unconfirmed reports that a plane has crashed into one of the towers of the World Trade Center."

Sucked into the television images, the bug man and I couldn't speak. We simply stood there, open-mouthed, making noises of horror and disbelief, watching the live footage of the devastation. I have no idea how long he lingered there watching the news with me, but at some point, he remembered he was working. He reminded me about the spray, and I nodded as if I heard him. I tried to call Lawrence, but the phone lines were already making the fast busy signal that meant they were down or overloaded.

I worried about my parents on their early morning flight from Florida to Chicago. It wasn't long before the news released the origination cities of the hijacked planes, so at least that worry was off the table. My second worry was did they get to Chicago before all air travel was suspended, or were they downed somewhere between Tampa and O'Hare? I tried to call, but those lines were down, too.

As I watched the towers fall in real time and then in slow motion over and over again, I was reminded of Pearl Harbor, Kristallnacht, the London Blitz and every other major event of the Second World War that began with a bang and issued in months of devastation and the march of millions to the death camps. My mind raced ahead to worst-case scenarios. Things were already shutting down—phones, airlines. What would be next? I knew there would be retaliation, but when? And would there be interruption of other services? Gas shortages? Food shortages?

I decided that working with Dante would focus my head on something more soothing and constructive, and perhaps other people whom we met as we did our normal training routine around the strip mall would appreciate the opportunity to pet the friendly dog and take a break from the insanity of the day. Before I could leave, Boo had to go out because he would most certainly have to go again before I got back from my errands. So out we went, forgetting all about the toxins on the deck and in the grass. As Boo peed, I suddenly remembered the bug man's warnings and grabbed Boo in a panic, running back into the house with him still streaming the last of his pee as we went. I wiped his paws and even up his legs very thoroughly to be sure he wouldn't lick any of the toxins off and poison himself.

Once we were on the road, Dante was happily riding along in his usual spot in the cab of the truck, with his unusually long tongue dangling out to one side. About ten minutes into the ride, I started feeling uncomfortable. My heart started racing, and I was sweating profusely. Then I realized I couldn't remember where I was taking Dante. I have enough trouble with directions in general that Lawrence painted markers on the trees on our property so I could find my way home when out on walks with the dogs, but this time my confusion was intense. Even looking back, I'm still not sure where I got off the highway or how I ended up driving into the parking lot of the Croton Falls Fire Department. The emergency workers, desperate to put their skills to use, descended on me like stretched-out rubber bands suddenly let loose as I stumbled my way out of the truck. I couldn't answer simple questions like my name or where I was going. On any other afternoon, I would have been asked who they could call, and that would have been that. On this day, they needed to help someone, and there I was, in need of some help.

The ambulance took me *and* Dante—he was happy to ride with me, sporting his goofy grin—to the emergency room nearby, and somebody got through to Lawrence. The emergency room was strangely empty that afternoon, and every emergency worker we ran into was frustrated by not being able to go directly to the fallen towers. They all badly needed to do something for someone, and in my confused, dazed way, I provided them with an outlet, at least for a moment in time. It turned out that when I'd wiped Boo's feet and legs clean of the bug man's poisons, I'd completely forgotten to wipe my own.

The hospital treated the toxins in my poisoned system with intravenous fluids and some juice. Dante, meanwhile, was the hit of the emergency room. Once the staff realized I was going to recover my senses, they started paying attention to him—sick people they saw every day, but Dante was something special. I had known he was going to do good work that day, but I just hadn't realized how. As I have come to expect from Boo, he set into motion that day—in his almost Gump-esque way—the chain of events that provided these folks with what they needed most: someone to save while they waited to be dispatched to Ground

Zero. By the time Lawrence got to the emergency room, my head had cleared, my heart was back to normal and I felt like an idiot. Embarrassment was a small price to pay for the chance to offer those emergency workers—frustrated and anxious that they couldn't be of more help where they were really needed—the relief that comes from the smile of a goofy dog and the tranquility that comes from petting the deep, inviting fur of an engaging animal.

I continued to think about our misadventure for the rest of the day and what a big stress reliever Dante had been for the emergency workers, and by that evening, Diane Pennington and I were talking about getting H.A.R.T. teams involved in some kind of therapeutic activity for the survivors, relief workers and families of the victims of 9/11. We didn't know yet what we would be doing, but like just about everyone else on the face of the planet, we knew we had to do something. We had trained dogs and teams that could provide relief, distraction and compassion, and I had seen firsthand how effectively Dante filled a need when he brightened the mood in the emergency room. We could only guess at what else our teams could bring to people trying to overcome this devastation, slogging their way through the nightmare that had just turned them emotionally inside out.

Just three years before, Pet Partners' teams were called in to assist the National Organization for Victim Assistance after the May 1998 Thurston High School shooting in Springfield, Oregon, that left four dead and two dozen injured. Cindy Ehlers (with her dog Bear) and Sandi Arrington (with her dog Garth) of Animal Assisted Crisis Response (AACR) broke ground by offering comfort and support to students, teachers and families in the wake of that tragedy. But AACR on the scale we were all considering was uncharted territory, so we figured our only option was to chart it.

Every year, more experts accept the effectiveness of visiting animals in therapeutic settings to ease emotional trauma. Animals can work with kids who are getting ready to testify against their parents in child abuse cases, calm college students under the pressures of finals, comfort cancer patients undergoing chemotherapy and act as assistants and sounding boards for clinical therapists treating patients with post-traumatic stress disorder. A 2008 study found that after patients with psychiatric disorders were teamed up with dogs, 84% reported that their symptoms improved, and 66% needed less medication. But in 2001, we had only the groundbreaking work of Cindy Ehlers and a few others to support our belief that we could help the families of 9/11 victims and the relief workers on site.

Within days, we partnered with neighboring visiting organizations, such as Hudson Valley Visiting Pet Program in Rockland County, Paw Prints on our Hearts in Putnam County, the Good Dog Foundation, the ASPCA (American Society for the Prevention of Cruelty to Animals), Dogs in Service in New Jersey and individuals like Liz Teal (my initial evaluator and mentor to many). All of us knew what our dogs could do in times of grief and other major emotional tumult in our own lives, and we had seen what they did on our regular visits to nursing homes, hospitals, psychiatric facilities, pediatric oncology wards and other similar venues. We scrambled into action like a hodgepodge of knitting circle/ fighter pilots on red alert.

As soon as the city announced the formation of the Family Assistance Center at Pier 94, we had a place to go. At the center, the Red Cross, along with other private and governmental organizations, was going to provide disaster relief for the families and loved ones of people lost in the Twin Towers and the planes. It was a brilliant, if macabre, way of bringing together all the support the survivors would need. Families could go there for help with searching for loved ones. If that search proved fruitless—as it unfortunately did for so many—they would then need help with requesting death certificates, insurance benefits and other social services.

Along with these practical services, families would also need emotional support—maybe someone to talk to, maybe someone for their kids to talk to or maybe someone for ongoing assistance. We suspected this would turn into a psychic black hole of epic size, but we were also certain our dogs could help keep some of these folks from spiraling into a vortex of depression as they adjusted to their new world.

The Family Assistance Center was going to be a place filled with such sorrow, anger, loss and confusion that we knew we needed specialized help to prepare the visiting teams. Few of us had ever prepared our dogs for anything like the huge emotions that they would face at the center. It was going to be vital for handlers to know their own emotional limitations to avoid burnout and also be able to support their dogs through the emotions they would be absorbing. Visiting dogs are like emotional sponges, and handlers needed a way to navigate these deep waters of grief so we could provide our animals for help and whatever assistance the actual trained therapists needed.

We asked Liz Teal and Maureen Fredrickson to help us all understand what our dogs might experience on this kind of visit and how we handlers could help and support them. Both Liz and Maureen were involved with Pet Partners from almost the very beginning; they were pioneers in shaping policies and the art of therapeutic visiting. By the Sunday after September 11, with Maureen and Liz in place, we had a room filled with eager handlers all chomping at the bit to go do something in the wake of the tragedy. We covered grieving, caregiver burnout, active listening and more. There wasn't a dry eye in the house when Liz told a story to drive home the point that it was the dogs themselves who often knew better than any of us humans what suffering people needed in the face of overwhelming emotions.

On the morning of September 11, Liz was out walking her dog in a lovely, manicured park in northern Manhattan when the towers were struck. On that blissfully sun-filled, early fall walk with her lovely Cavalier King Charles spaniel, Annie, Liz knew nothing about the events happening several miles south of her. Passing an older man on a park bench, she noticed he was bent over what looked like an old transistor radio. Not thinking too much of this, she continued on her walk, but Annie had other ideas. The little fourteen-pound dog pulled insistently toward the man on the bench. Liz wondered what could make an otherwise good, loose-leash-walking dog like Annie behave in such an anomalous manner, but she knew, from years of working with various animals in a visiting setting, to trust the animal, so she let her dog lead her to the man. The sweet little Cavalier jumped with fluid motion onto the bench, and the older man's arms, with an equally fluid motion, wrapped themselves automatically around the petite dog. As he huddled with her, he began weeping. Still unaware of what was happening, Liz sat down with the stranger as he snuggled Annie and continued crying into the silken fur of this patient little creature.

Liz's understanding came in horrible pieces. First, she noticed the tattooed numbers on his arm, and she wondered what could make this man, a Nazi death camp survivor, weep with such ferocity. She wondered, Has he lost someone? Was it an anniversary that only he knew, the birthday of a lost loved one, or the day he was liberated? Liz couldn't ask for details; she could only wait until he seemed more composed. As if in response to her unspoken questions, he turned up the radio and held it out so she could hear the explanation that was muffled in his coat and Annie's fur. The two of them sat together, weeping for the current tragedy and the tragedies of the past, while Annie did her best to keep them both grounded in what is good and joyful in the human–animal bond.

Listening to Liz tell this story, I wondered if Dante was the right dog for the Family Assistance Center. I was torn between knowing that as a bounding, ebullient tongue bandito who licked first and asked questions later, this whirling dervish of a dog might do wonders for many at the center; but maybe a quieter dog was better suited for this venue. Regardless of his aptitude for this work, he was almost six and was showing signs that his hip dysplasia was starting to affect him. The sixty-plus-mile drive to the Family Assistance Center was something he would do if I asked him to, but for dogs with joint issues, driving can be painful, as the act of balancing when the car turns, stops and starts puts a lot of pressure on the joints. Since I had already discovered Dante's hip dysplasia when he began to falter on his favorite Scooby Doo trick, I didn't want him to endure that kind of pain and discomfort on the way to the pier. I couldn't sign him up for these visits.

Dogs are infamous for their lack of display when they are in minor to moderate pain, so it's often hard to tell whether they are. We've all seen our dogs run headfirst into a coffee table or other solid object, only to walk it off. A similar situation for humans would result in much howling and cursing, or at the very least a pause in activity. Some people take dogs' stoic reaction to pain as permission to use harsh training methods—if they don't feel it, then it can't hurt, right? The reality, though, is that they *do* feel it. There are measurable and fairly standard chemical responses to pain, both in dogs and humans. Dogs are probably more stoic than humans when it comes to pain simply because it's not advantageous for them to display pain as radically as humans do. A dog who is injured while hunting for dinner and stops to say, "Owie!" will lose her dinner. If she wants to eat, she has to keep moving and check her pain until later. Our dogs' ethology (animal behavior) is altogether different from ours: a quiet dog isn't necessarily a pain-free dog, and a growling, snarling, barking dog might be responding to pain rather than displaying territorial or other types of aggression. In the end, no dog in unmanaged or undetermined pain should be working. This is a setup for mistakes as minor as simply blowing off a client or as major as growling, snapping or biting.

Giving Dante a break, I went on the Family Assistance Center visits as a team leader with the teams from H.A.R.T. Programs and worked to help Diane as a co–program leader. As a team leader, I was in a unique position to observe what these dogs were doing for the people inside the center. My job was to accompany a team made up of one handler and one dog as their support. If they needed to get through a crowd, it was my job to part the waters. If clients were monopolizing the team, it was my job to interrupt and say the dog was needed elsewhere but would be back later. If something was happening with a client that could not be interrupted, it was my job to let others know that the team would be delayed. I was also on lookout—it's amazing what people will sometimes do to a dog, especially in a very stressful situation.

There was plenty for me to look out for at the Family Assistance Center as we were met by folks in need as soon as teams arrived at the entrance. Every Red Cross worker who had to leave a dog at home needed the affection of one of our visiting dogs. Even the typically stoic military police at the entrances and checkpoints got into the dogs.

"Ooh, what a nice dog," one remarked.

"I had one just like that!" exclaimed another. "Can I pet your dog?"

The officers' high-pitched, talking-to-dog voices were positively gooey.

Clearly, these support personnel were in as much need as the family members who had lost someone. I couldn't help smiling when I remembered how my accidental poisoning had helped inspire my being there. It was almost as if Boo, the piddling puppy, sent Dante and me in a predetermined direction that day.

Because I knew firsthand just how important these dogs could be for the workers as well as the families, when the support personnel asked if they could pet the dogs, I always answered with a resounding yes. Our teams knew they would be working from the moment they entered the facility because each person they encountered would probably need the kind touch of a visiting dog. Everyone who was in proximity to the events of 9/11 has stories. Some are horrible remembrances of unspeakable trauma, but for us, visiting with our dogs at the Family Assistance Center, the stories are about the palpable emotions that people wore like heavy, wet clothing and how the interactions with our dogs seemed to lighten that burden a little. The unconditional love that dogs give us allows us to see them as pure in the face of our tragedies and sorrows and allows us to use them like a sponge to soak up those emotions. Although they don't fix the problem, they can give us a moment of Zen. We remove ourselves from the tumult to ease our blood pressures and our souls as we feel the warm fur of a friendly, comforting animal against our fingers.

Diane and I also collected post-visit reports from the teams. Probably one of the greatest follow-up reports came from Diane herself and her wonderful golden, Hunter.

Two weeks after the Twin Towers fell, Diane and Hunter were in the kids' corner at the Family Assistance Center with Bobbie, a little boy who still hadn't spoken a word about the loss of his father. Bobbie's mother and the staff were reasonably worried about him. Busy drawing when Hunter entered with Diane, Bobbie saw them and put down his crayons to go see the lovely eighty-plus pounds of smiling, golden-coated fringe.

"What's his name?" Bobbie asked.

"Hunter," said Diane.

"How old is he?"

"Just about three," she answered.

"What kind of dog is he?" Bobbie kept on asking question after question.

Diane realized Bobbie was probably going to exhaust even her knowledge of Hunter, so she suggested, "Would you like to take Hunter for a walk?"

Bobbie was up and ready for his walk as he said yes, then remembered to check in with his mother.

Diane said to them both, "We can all go together."

When we do a "stranger" walk with our dogs on a visit, the client takes the handle of the leash while the handler maintains control over the dog by holding the center of the leash. This allows the handler to be a buffer to prevent any unwanted tension on the dog's collar or harness and keeps the dog from tripping or pulling the client. It was impossible for Bobbie and his mom to walk around the Family Assistance Center with a big, beautiful, friendly dog without being stopped. As folks asked about the gorgeous dog, Diane directed their questions to Bobbie, who by this time knew quite a bit about Hunter and could tell them where he liked to be petted ("just here on the side of his neck") and how he liked his treats ("slobbery").

Finally, after Bobbie introduced Hunter to all his adoring fans, Bobbie turned to Diane. "Can I take him to the wall of bears?" he asked.

Diane encouraged him by replying, "You're in charge. Take us where you'd like to go."

"It's over there," he said as he guided the team to the wall.

The wall of bears was one of the most heart-rending things I have ever seen: a wall almost a city block long of teddy bears for loved ones, pictures of the missing and notes of love and remembrances. Once there, Bobbie walked directly to the picture of his father and said to Hunter, "That's a picture of my dad. That's my dad."

Diane answered for Hunter, "I see—that's your dad." Bobbie's mother began to cry, Diane gave up trying not to and soon everybody was crying.

"It's okay, Mom," said Bobbie, still holding Hunter's leash. "It'll be okay."

Diane says she remembers thinking two things at that moment: *When will it be okay?* and *What a great kid, comforting his mother like that!* Bobbie continued to walk Hunter around the center, proudly answering any and all questions about the dog. For that hour, Bobbie's job as the Hunter answer man allowed him to forget, a little bit, about his family's loss.

No one can say whether Bobbie would have spoken about losing his dad that night without Hunter's presence, but we know that Hunter made things a little easier for everyone in Bobbie's family.

Once the AACR work at the Family Assistance Center was finished, many of the local groups began to work together to set down some solid protocols and procedures to keep AACR dogs safe and to offer training and resources for teams who wanted to be ready for the next crisis whose survivors might be well served by visiting-dog teams.

As the effort to codify crisis response went on, I spent as much time on it as I could, but I still had Boo, who needed potty-training and beyond. Meanwhile, Dante and I were visiting more and more—adults with developmental disabilities, seniors in a nursing home setting, adult clients in a day-care facility and the Westchester Board of Cooperative Educational Services (BOCES) in Armonk. This particular BOCES facility taught kids who had multiple disabilities, ranging from toddlers to teenagers. It was a forty-five-minute drive, which was about as much as Dante and I could take before we were both in too much pain to work. The drive was worth it, though. The facility people there were terrific guides when we were interacting with the kids, so it was easy to see who needed what from the dogs, clear who was happy to see the dogs and who wasn't, and in the end, possible to do actual therapeutic visiting under the direction of therapists.

It was at BOCES that I began to understand the extent of dogs' power to reach even the seemingly most unreachable. On one visit, a physical therapist brought a beautiful two-year-old boy who was blind and deaf out to see Dante. She explained to me that children born deaf and blind are often reluctant to unclench their fists, and she wanted to see whether petting a dog would allow him to relax enough to open his hands. She cradled the child on her lap on the floor while I sat next to Dante, who was down in a one-hip-over position, flat on his side on the floor. The therapist held the little boy's hands and gently stroked Dante's belly. In the large recreation room where we were trying to have this calm, serene visit, zany time went on all around us as dozens of other children played on swings, rode tricycles, pushed and bounced big physioballs and sang music. It was a setting in which it was very hard for Dante to just lay down and not engage with any of the distractions, but he was taking this very seriously. Because it was hard for this little boy to demonstrate any emotion, all we could really look for was the unclenching of his fists, but this didn't happen.

"Do you think . . ." said the therapist eventually, embarrassed, as if she were asking for money. "I mean, would Dante mind if Joey petted him with his feet?"

"Of course not," I said. "He's a dog. He loves that."

Since Dante was already lying quietly on his side, I just moved a little closer to his head so the therapist would have more room to maneuver the boy's feet and legs. She removed his shoes and rubbed his toes against the shepherd-mix's deep chest and belly while I whispered into Dante's ear that this was all good and he was doing a great job.

Little by little, the child's tight, rigid muscles began to relax. Even Dante seemed to drift off for a little bit as the boy's whole body became soft and tranquil. After a few minutes, the boy opened his hands and rested them on Dante, one on his hind legs and one on his shoulder. The therapist was thrilled. Nothing else she had ever tried had relaxed the child enough to unclench his hands, and Dante managed it in minutes. I was amazed. I also marveled at Dante's ability to suppress all his natural instincts in a chaotic recreation room full of kids, bikes, swings, music, and as Dr. Seuss would say, noise, noise, noise, noise. He simply lay there quietly for the little boy who needed him. After such a touching moment, Dante just got up and engaged in zany antics with the other kids, as that's what they needed of him.

It isn't just the clients who receive a gift when an animal team visits. The caregivers, the handlers and probably even the dogs all feel a connection with other living beings who care and are there for just them at that moment. It is one of the greatest gifts of love we can give one another.

It had been ten years since Atticus had come into my life to show me what the human–animal bond could do to heal. Then, it was Dante's turn to bring me further understanding of how dogs could heal by teaching me more about dogs, dog language and training skills. But what about Boo?

7
Class Dunce
Makes Good

Part of me wished that Boo could follow in Dante's oversized and comical footsteps, but whenever I considered training Boo to be a therapy dog, I kept returning to the stark reality of his slow progress in learning any reliable foundation skills. I doubted his ability to pass the Pet Partners' evaluation, let alone handle the higher levels of distractions that the work itself would present.

No, Boo was destined to be simply a very loved, very pampered pet whose favorite place to sleep was in bed nestled between Lawrence and me in a position we called the snug-a-Boo. (I'm certain a good number of deep gasps greeted the revelation that my dogs are allowed up on our bed. The usual reason given for keeping dogs off furniture—it makes them aggressive or dominant—isn't supported by research; in fact, there is evidence to the contrary. A survey of 2,000 dog owners conducted by Drs. Peter Borchelt and Linda Goodloe, both veterinary behaviorists, showed no correlation between sleeping on furniture and aggression; it also debunked a few other dog myths. Dogs who are allowed up on the furniture, however, need to have a verbal off command and a great settle command. The first night your dog goes out to perform some kind of proctology exam on the local skunks, as Dante used to, you will be *thrilled* you can tell him to get off the bed and go lie down somewhere else—preferably far away from you!) Between us, Boo would press himself against one of us (snug-a-Boo) and reach out with his feet to push against the other (poky-Boo). Snug-a-Boo was a truly marvelous way to fall asleep—face buried in thick, warm Boo fur—while the one receiving poky-Boo woke up the next day with a back full of pointy, little Boo paw prints.

Nevertheless, I still needed Boo to be socialized and well trained. By now, he was pretty good at tagging along with me on a reasonably loose leash. The only exceptions came when he saw a person or another dog, at which point he became a plow—so intent on reaching his goal that no bag of peanut butter could distract him. One evening as we left the store after I had just finished teaching, Boo, who had come along just for the social outing, was prancing along nicely beside me when he suddenly started pulling in the opposite direction, with no people or other dogs in sight. Ordinarily, I would have just kept walking, perhaps giving the leash a little tug, until he was back with me, but this night his behavior baffled me, and I decided to let him follow his bliss. He steamrolled past two aisles, turned down the third one and plowed ahead to the middle of the aisle.

There, halfway down the third aisle, were two giggling little girls, probably about three and four years old, huddled together in a Dickensian sort of pose, pointing at Boo as he beelined for them. Boo did not have much experience with kids, so I tried to slow him down, but he was a dog on a mission, an unstoppable force, until he reached the girls, at which point he stopped dead in his tracks, turned his body slightly, opened his mouth for a gentle pant and just stood there, as the giggling girls proceeded to poke him, pet him, grab him, prod him and eventually hug him.

I was in shock. This was not the Boo who was usually a whirligig at the end of the leash when hoping to get the attention of people and other dogs. It wasn't just that this was really good behavior—this was behavior that usually required an *extraordinary* amount of training. When you're a small child, the sight of a dog the same size as you, or bigger, bounding directly at you can be terrifying or really fun. No matter which, the child usually beams excitement through the air to the dog, communicating, *Oh boy, let's play!* or *Oh no!* Even dogs who remain calm around adults can have a hard time not getting overly excited around kids, which can lead to the potential for injury. Dante, the prodigal dog, still had trouble moderating his exuberance around little kids. I'd been working with him for years to make his small-child greeting consistently soft and gentle, but Boo, running on instinct alone, with no shaping, luring or training, blew the genius dog out of the water. I almost broke down in tears. Boo was telling me exactly and unequivocally what he needed and wanted in his life: kids!

I wasn't sure I could give him that, as Lawrence and I weren't going to have children. Knowing that abuse follows from one generation to the next, Lawrence believed the best way to keep himself from becoming his biological father—maybe the only way—was to avoid having kids. His early childhood had been so dark that even the remote possibility that he might inflict a portion of that darkness on another child terrified him. I also knew that the combination of my medical history and his newly discovered medical issues made it unlikely we'd be able to produce a child no matter how much Boo and I wanted one. I had long since realized that my life would bring me what it was going to bring me and that there was no requesting special-menu items. I was just amazed that I had found someone to marry me in the first place. I figured that if children were going to sneak their way into this family, it would be at the discretion of a higher power.

With no kids on the horizon at home, all I could do was try to get Boo to a point where he could be a visiting dog like Dante. Then, he could have as many kids as he could visit. The problem would be training Boo so he could pass the Pet Partners' evaluation. There were probably never two more dramatically different dogs than Dante and Boo. Dante, smart as a whip, trained so easily that much of the time I felt like he was the one training me. But with Boo, the not so smart one, training sometimes seemed like trying to train a two-by-four. Dante, smart, empathic and energetic, could be a clown on one visit— employing his special Scooby Doo trick that always amused everyone as they watched him barely balance his ninety pounds on his two hind legs, his ears flopping as the rest of him wobbled—and then on another visit he could intuit the right thing to do while still keeping his focus on me and following my commands. Boo, on the contrary, had trouble focusing even without distractions, and it remained to be seen whether he could perceive the needs of clients at all: were his low-key, easygoing interactions an expression of empathy or just a function of his disabilities?

I had reason to hope because little Boo was

making progress in his training when out and about with me at work, and he wasn't making potty mistakes in the house anymore. He had learned how to signal to us that he needed to go out. This was the longest it had ever taken me to get a dog to be 100% potty-trained, but I found it encouraging. If Boo could make training headway in this, then maybe the other skills necessary to be a therapy dog were also within his reach.

But, as always, my hope was offset by my worry that Boo, with his limitations, might be more fearful than the average dog. So, knowing that happy socialization was especially important for him, I made sure to bring him to work with me even more often now. This enabled me to proof his foundation skills and generalize them in increasingly distracting environments. (Proofing is the act of determining the quality of a behavior through testing it in various environments; this also strengthens the behaviors and generalizes them to all situations.) It wasn't enough for him to sit on command at home; he needed to be able to sit on command anywhere.

Dogs don't generalize like we humans do. If you're in a classroom and teach a child that $2 + 2 = 4$, she understands that $2 + 2 = 4$ wherever she goes, whoever's asking. If kids had the same approach to learning as dogs do, childhood education would look something like this:

Day one: $2 + 2 = 4$.

Day two: $4 + 4 = 8$.

Day three: Field trip! In the mall parking lot, $2 + 2 = 4$. In the candle store, $2 + 2 = 4$. In the furniture store, $2 + 2 = 4$. In the food court, $2 + 2 = 4$.

Day four: Field trip! In the mall parking lot, $4 + 4 = 8$, and once again in the candle store, the furniture store and the food court.

Day five: Field trip to a *different* mall! In the parking lot, $2 + 2 = 4$ and $4 + 4 = 8$. Then, in *this* mall's candle store, furniture store and food court, $2 + 2 = 4$ and $4 + 4 = 8$.

You get the picture. It's time-consuming, but it's the only reliable way to ensure solid, generalized commands.

Thanks to my happy discovery of the peanut butter puppet, Boo was actually making progress for the first time. Before, he would sit on command at home but never in class, but now he would often sit for practice sessions between my classes at the pet store and sometimes even in other places! Even more exciting, once he'd gotten into the groove of a new place and had a few licks of peanut butter, he would start taking regular treats, which were much easier to carry and much less messy. For the first time, I had the ability to shape, lure and reward targeted behaviors. I was thrilled. It's a funny thing how our expectations shift: in the beginning, I had long lists of things I needed him to do, and now he could make me incredibly happy by sitting on command in a mildly distracting environment.

Although happy to be working on my new goal for Boo, I never stopped twinging inside whenever I thought of my failure to prepare him for Chuck. The last twinge was put to rest in May 2002, when Boo was one and a half and the call came. Like in the middle of a dream when someone familiar enters a scene they don't normally belong in, I got a call from my sister. Once again following strict Edwards family rules of engagement, all she said was, "Lees, Chuck's dead," and then gave me details on the funeral. I left Lawrence and the boys home and went back to Lombard for what I figured would be the last time. I would normally have stayed with Chuck and his family, but that didn't feel right. My sister and her husband begrudgingly put me up. Still trying to ingratiate myself with her, I helped them mulch their yard before the funeral service and took them out to dinner afterward. But no matter what I did, the old feeling of "Don't let the door hit your ass on the way out" hung in the air, heavy and impenetrable.

I got to spend some time with Chuck's family before leaving, and his wife told me that when she and my niece had come home to find that Chuck had passed, he was sitting in front of the

TV, which was turned to the sci-fi channel. She laughed and said, "That's my Chuck." I got goose bumps. I had taken that day off and spent it watching the sci-fi channel while working on a sewing project. My brother was gone, but it gave me solace to know that we were probably watching the same *Babylon 5* episode when he died.

For me, the loss of someone important churns my internal emotional waters, reminding me to keep important things important and not let them get pushed aside by other pressures. At Chuck's funeral, his wife read aloud a letter he wrote about what he would have done if the illness had not taken him: hug his daughter more, plant tomatoes in his garden and hand-build cabinets for his kitchen. After I got home from the funeral, I thought, *You know what? My kitchen has been in pieces ever since Boo came along, and a halfway demolished cabinet was his first playpen. If Chuck's illness gave me a reason to work with Boo toward a specific goal, I can let his death inspire me to work toward a goal, too.* Chuck and I shared science fiction and woodworking. I shared his last moments, even if half a country away, and now I would make that kitchen an homage to him while I focused the energy of my grief on creating something tangible. I thought, *I'm finishing that kitchen, come hell or high water.* My approach to anything negative is to keep busy, so the pieces of the puzzle that would allow me to process my grief were to finish the kitchen and work toward my dog training certifications. If Chuck could get his CPA facing a fatal illness, then I had no excuse to not get my professional certifications, no matter how inadequate I felt.

Committing to renovate the kitchen while training Boo and pursuing certification was one thing. Actually *doing* it—conquering the kitchen while continuing to work with Boo and trying to slog through heady learning theory reading material made doubly heady by dyslexia—was something else altogether. We slogged through the kitchen prep work, and once I'd designed the space, laid the in-floor heating and the tile above it and moved the new appliances, it was time for the cabinets to arrive.

In preparation for the delivery, I put Atticus and Dante up in the bedroom, but I kept Boo downstairs as a greeter to continue his social-ization by introducing him to as many people as possible.

The delivery guys loved Boo. He made an excellent supervisor, trotting his pony-like trot, ears flopping with each step, following them around the house as they brought in box after box to make sure they put everything in the right place, until he decided that he needed to be involved in more of the process and began following them outside to the truck and back in again. Seeing him so consistently engaged, I allowed myself to focus more of my attention on the seemingly never-ending stream of boxes entering my house—boxes six feet high, boxes four feet wide—trying to find a place for the next box that would still leave us some house to live in. Before too long, I was completely engrossed in the problem: my house is small, and there were a *lot* of boxes.

When the men were gone, I called for Boo, but he didn't come. I searched every room with no luck. I let Atticus and Dante out and figured they'd find him in the maze of boxes, but still no Boo. We headed outside to search the property. Still no Boo.

"I'm sorry to bother you," I said to the driver of the truck when he answered his cell phone, "but there wouldn't by any chance be an unauthorized canine passenger with you, would there?"

"No, ma'am," he said. "The truck was definitely empty when we closed it up."

I called Lawrence at work in a panic. He dropped everything and headed home to help look for our lost little guy. Boo had been gone for at least a half hour at this point, and with his vision issues and cognitive disabilities, he could have wandered anywhere on our ten acres, or anywhere else in the neighborhood, and have no hope of finding his way home. I was trying not to panic. Boo always ran from the sound of cars, but what if he ran from one car only to charge head on into another one? It was time to go driving around the neighborhood and hope to find him still alive. Our house is up a long shared easement about a quarter mile from the road, surrounded at the bottom by woods and a bit of a swamp, most of which is owned by New York City for watershed protection.

Driving down the easement, as I neared the road at the bottom, I saw a small, very dark deer in the swampy portion of the watershed swamp-land. As I drew closer, I realized it was not a deer but little Boo, happily and nonchalantly sniffing all the new wonderful smells in the swamp. Overjoyed, I went running and screaming into the swamp. I must have looked ridiculous, with my arms waving and flailing about. I picked Boo up and carried him back to the car. In that moment, I realized I was running, I was carrying Boo and I was throwing myself around like a windmill. These were activities that I thought I couldn't do anymore because of the pain. I was a little sore, but not like so many nights I had spent under bags of ice.

The combination of less time spent pounding my joints on New York City pavement and more time spent moving through the pain when teaching classes, as well as the extra time on my feet working with Boo, must have all played a huge therapeutic role in my increased mobility and decreased chronic pain. Although I was not completely pain-free, I was doing things I hadn't done in years. I could spend time on my feet as a part-time dog trainer, usually at least two hours in a row. I was also sharing more of the responsibilities for teaching the main H.A.R.T. class—another two hours of being on my feet—and the visit hours. This made four to six hours each week that I was up and about, moving and being moderately active. Because I loved the activity, my brain could overlook the pain. I was experiencing the benefits of animal therapy firsthand.

The revelations I had on the day we almost lost Boo allowed me to step outside myself and watch while I taught and trained and did demonstrations for H.A.R.T. For the first time, I realized that maybe these people who kept telling me I was good at this dog-training thing weren't making it up. By wandering off during the cabinet delivery, Boo allowed me to see something in myself that I hadn't known was there. I was no longer the same cripple I had been when I needed a neck brace and the stick just to get to and from work in the city. Maybe I could manage a job that required some physical activity. And maybe I would actually be really good at it.

I was so fiercely trained to believe I was worthless that it was difficult for me to keep hold of this understanding. But my stubborn streak showed itself, and before long I decided that I could earn the credentials that would allow me to call myself a professional, and there would be no argument from anybody.

To that point, the decisions I'd made about dog training—with Boo and with other dogs—had come from light reading and instinct. My own history made me doubt that training through punishment (collar corrections, pinch collars, shock collars) could do much to build a trusting relationship between dog and handler. I knew punishment training wasn't an effective training tool for me, and I suspected it probably wouldn't be for dogs either.

As I began to study, I discovered that my instinct was supported by science. I read every book on learning theory, operant conditioning, classical conditioning, clicker training, behavior modification, desensitization and counter-conditioning that I could get my hands on. I learned that research on how lab animals respond to positive punishment (pain, fear, etc.) and positive reinforcement (rewards of food, play, affection) showed not just that my intuition was right but also that there were chemical reasons why.

The neurological responses in the brain and

body to fear and pain fall into the general category of stress responses. The neurochemicals and hormones produced by moderate to high levels of stress impair learning (unless we're talking about hand-in-the-fire pain and stress, which is a very powerful learning process, but that isn't dog training). The techniques of positive reinforcement, however, don't create those high levels of stress hormones, but they do create chemicals associated with happiness. Both of these factors make learning more likely, more efficient and more reliable in the long term.

I already belonged to the Association of Pet Dog Trainers, which spun off an adjunct organization, the Certification Council for Professional Dog Trainers, founded for the sole purpose of testing and certifying the knowledge base of trainers nationwide while supporting a venue for pet-dog owners to learn about and find these certified trainers. I took the CPDT (certified professional dog trainer) test through the Certification Council for Professional Dog Trainers when Boo was two years old. I must have been crazy: it was a 250-question exam that tested knowledge of learning theory, ethology, training techniques, equipment and husbandry. To even sit for the test, a trainer had to have three hundred hours of verifiable independent training experience as a lead or sole trainer, along with references from clients, colleagues and veterinary professionals. Several seasoned trainers I knew had taken it time and again only to fail and have to retest.

I passed the first time. Maybe I was good at dog-training after all.

I was now a nationally certified dog trainer, and there was no stopping me. I quickly became an American Kennel Club–certified Canine Good Citizen (CGC) evaluator, a Pet Partners-certified instructor, a Pet Partners-certified evaluator, you name it. By the time Boo was two and a half, I was a professional dog trainer with all the credentials one could ask for to be taken seriously: CPDT, AKC CGC certified evaluator and Pet Partners certified instructor and evaluator. Most of these letters and titles don't mean much to folks outside the dog-training community, but to me and to people in the doggie world, they meant I was legitimate and probably pretty knowledgeable. It was time to formally start my company. Paying homage to all the dogs who had brought me so much, I called it Three Dogs Training.

Now that I sort of felt like I knew what I was doing—and had the credentials to back up that knowledge—I started Boo's training over again. It was much like the first round for service training had been, with great emphasis on socialization and generalized behaviors, but this time my expectations were more in line with what he could do. I knew his strengths (people) and his weaknesses (learning new skills). I had to begin working with his strengths and then slowly lure him into the skills category.

Boo had an exceptional ability to gently and disarmingly say hello to a small child and then just stand there (the old Boo stare was finally given a purpose!) while the child petted him, cooed, tried to braid his hair or played cowboys and Indians with him. It was just like the days when he would be outside staring into the wind with a look of confused glee, but when kids were petting him, I knew the source of his glee: the love and affection he was getting and giving. As kids in stores and parks petted him, he remained relaxed, mouth gently open for calm, happy panting, without jumping or moving in too close to startle or scare the child and always with his body slightly curved in the midsection, a sure sign of relaxation (in contrast, when dogs are on alert their bodies are usually straight and ridged). For many kids, Boo was the one dog they could pet. Because he wasn't bouncing all over the place trying to lick them or paw at them, he wasn't scary at all. For other kids, he was just good company. Boo really *was* the dog who would let kids nudge him, poke him and pet him anywhere—that rare dog every parent dreams about. (It is important to remember that the phrase "I want a dog who will let my kids do anything to him" is a description of a very rare dog. It's unrealistic and dangerous to expect all dogs to tolerate everything kids will do to them. Without training, shaping and management, many dogs will eventually try to tell children to stop doing something in the only ways they can, by growling, barking or snapping at the child.)

It took nearly another year of specialized training for Boo before I felt he was ready for the Human–Animal Relational Therapies class. Diane and I took turns teaching the main H.A.R.T. Animal-Assisted Therapy class at this point, and since it was Diane's turn to teach, I enrolled Boo. I would be able to devote all my class efforts to him and just be a student again, something I hadn't done in a long time. As usual, I spent a good deal of time in class just getting him to focus his attention on me rather than the other dogs. It was not as hard as before—my bubble sounds were much less frequent this time—but it was still a good deal of work.

The real difference was that I was no longer beating myself up when Boo didn't progress quickly. I simply worked with him at his speed. If we had to do this class over and over again, we would, and I was fine with that. Boo taught me how to be patient and let things go at the pace that was required. It was a humbling and empowering lesson. Although things may be out of our control in many ways, we have the power to let them be what they must be over time. Boo brought me back to the Serenity Prayer I learned in Al-Anon: "God grant me the serenity to accept the things I cannot change, courage to change the things I can and wisdom to know the difference." The power of this fifth-century prayer to transform and inform was never lost on me.

Every day when training Boo, the Boo form of that prayer would go through my head: I knew I could never change Boo into the bright intellectual canine wizard that Dante was, yet I knew I could get him to become a therapy dog if I just kept working with him. I just needed to put in the time and have patience.

The Animal-Assisted Therapy, Education and Activities (AATEA) class that Diane and I taught for H.A.R.T.—and now teach for Three Dogs Training—is an intensive class that prepares teams for any evaluation and the work they will eventually do for the two types of animal-assisted visiting: animal-assisted activities (AAA) and animal-assisted therapy (AAT). I also like to include a third category, animal-assisted education.

AAA is the most common type of animal-assisted visiting. The most familiar type of AAA visit is a dog at a person's bedside in a hospital or nursing home. The staff and client don't expect anything more than a friendly dog to come by and brighten up the morning, maybe reduce some blood pressure and generally make everyone smile a little more. Although AAA visits are not prescribed by medical professionals and do not require progress notes, they bring enormous therapeutic benefits.

AAT, on the contrary, is a visit during which the client and the dog engage in monitored, goal-driven, professionally prescribed therapeutic interactions whose progress is documented from visit to visit. For example, if an occupational therapist would like a client to work on range of motion for an arm that has been injured, she might ask the client to brush the visiting dog twenty times with his right hand and then with his left. Or if another client is working on fine-motor skills, they might play games like Don't Spill the Beans with the visiting dog. Once the client puts a pile of beans into the pot one by one, the dog is cued to tip over the pot, dumping all the beans out, so the client can start over. Yes, a staff member could push over the pot, but it's more fun when dogs do it.

Last, there's animal-assisted education. Most folks classify educational visits as AAA, but on many classroom visits I've done, a teacher directs the activities with individualized goals and documented progress notes for each student, just as a reading specialist might oversee the progress a child is making each time she reads a book to the dog. These visits seemed more like AAT to me.

The next step was to get Boo ready for the Pet Partners' evaluation. If he passed, I would register him as a pet partner, or therapy dog. The test has two parts: skills and aptitude. A team has to pass all ten exercises in the skills portion in order to go onto the aptitude portion. On this test, each exercise is scored as follows: a team can score 2 (the best possible), 1 (fine), NR (not ready) or NA (not appropriate as a pet partner ever). The test basically requires a doggie Gandhi—intelligent, caring, patient and empathic. I had Boo.

After a few months, we finished our class, and it was time to test. The evaluator, Liz, knew me and respected me—she evaluated Dante and me the first couple of times—so she was a little shocked when she saw Boo. I could see her eyes squint just a bit as she did the comparison in her head between my whiz-kid Dante and Boo. It didn't matter because Boo was going to be who he was.

The first time, the skills test alone stressed him enough that he didn't manage to do his basic commands, and we didn't pass. I had expected that, and back to work we went. We went to pet stores and the vet's office, and some dry cleaners and other small shop owners let us in. In each venue, we ran through the basic exercises in the skills portion of the test, sometimes in order, sometimes out of order. I wasn't going to give up yet.

As Boo's training continued, his world at home was getting better. For one thing, his relationship with Atticus was improving. Their favorite game was played out in the yard: Boo would stand very still and eye Atticus. Atticus would stand equally still and eye Boo. I could almost hear the music from *The Good, the Bad and the Ugly* playing in my head as they made their standoff like Clint Eastwood (or in this case, Eastwoof) and Eli Wallach. Then, in a short sudden movement, one of them would quickly pitch forward and down, then lean in the direction the chase was supposed to go, and they would be off like a shot, running circles around each other and weaving in and out of the trees in the yard, their faces happy and open, tongues wagging and bodies wriggly. At some point, Boo would stop and give up his typical, "Whoo, whoo, whoo," howling-at-the-moon bark in his coyote-like stance, and the game would wind down. Once inside, they would engage in their mutual passion: begging (I use begging to shape and proof good behaviors). Atticus and Boo were the dynamic duo of sitting politely for any treat at all. After a long day of chasing and buddy-begging, Boo would frequently split his evenings between snoozing on the couch in my office with Atticus and snuggling with Dante and me on the oversized chair in the living room.

More important, though, Lawrence finally seemed to have found his place with Boo, too. Although Boo's slow responsiveness still frustrated Lawrence, I noticed a definite shift when I started telling him about the folks in the H.A.R.T. class.

"They called Boo a dullard during class again," I said.

"Who?" His eyes narrowed.

"The usual crew. I'm not sure they were joking. When I try to explain his limitations, I think they think I'm making it all up."

"They," he said indignantly, "just don't know Boo."

That proved to be a turning point. The more he heard about the jokes, the more he rooted for Boo to succeed in the class and show the snickering strangers how wrong they were. This was *not* the man who had said, "Fine, but he's *your* dog. I'm not taking care of him." This was a man who was growing to love a dog he never thought he wanted.

Just a little over a year after Chuck's passing, Boo took the Pet Partners' test again. Our evaluators

189

this time were Kay and another Diane (Anderson).
They were enrolled in the first class I helped
teach with Dante, and once they became
evaluators, they did evaluations for H.A.R.T.
Again, it wasn't hard to see them compare Dante
with this little black dog who seemed to float at
the end of his leash with no focus on me and not
hard to see their shock at the obvious differences
between the two. As a horrible test taker in
general, I was more worried on this occasion
than usual. Boo and I had failed once. What if we
failed again and again and again? At what point
would I have to step back and ask whether this
was good for Boo? On some gut level, I knew
what an amazing therapy dog Boo could be, and
I wanted this so badly for him.

"Breathe, Lisa," Kay said more than once as
we went through the exercises.

"You're so stressed," Diane said at one point,
"that you keep inhaling and holding your breath.
Let it out." Boo, meanwhile, was his usual,
unfocused self through the skills portion of the
test, only occasionally turning to look at me
when I gave him a command.

"Down" was going to be our make-or-break
exercise—our doom, or we would be home free.
Boo always had trouble lying down easily even
under the best of circumstances, and it was
almost painful to watch sometimes. He couldn't
lie down normally because of the cerebellar

hypoplasia. Furthermore, on a hard floor, he slipped and slid around under his own weight, unable to get his front legs out easily. He hated the down command on a hard surface, but there was no missing any of the skills exercises: we had to pass them all, or we wouldn't pass the evaluation.

As always, the test began slowly with Diane approaching for the first two exercises: "Accepting a Stranger" and "Accepting Petting." Boo was interested in greeting Diane but managed to remain at my side for my hand-shake and Diane's petting him. Following the greeting, Diane brushed him and touched him all over just a bit to be sure he was comfortable being touched by a stranger ("Appearance and Grooming"). Happy to be petted and touched, Boo seemed confused as to why he couldn't interact more with his new friend, but we had other exercises to get through first. It was time for "Go for a Walk." Boo trotted along with me past the cones, leash loose, ears flopping happily as usual, without corrections like collar tugs or stern verbal instructions. Now that we had proven that we could walk politely on leash, the volunteers entered the picture ("Walk Through a Crowd"). Boo and I had to navigate through the crowd milling about without his being overly interested or fearful of the strangers passing by.

"Reaction to Distractions" followed, and Boo didn't care about the person moving quickly with a walker in our path (or maybe he just didn't see her). As the clipboard hit the floor for the audio distraction, Boo turned (as did the rest of the room), but I jollied him, and he recovered like a champ.

We had reached Boo's make-or-break point, as the next four exercises included the dreaded "Down" (the sit wasn't going to come too easily either). "Sit," I said, working my cup-of-tea voice (the tone of voice, as Diane Pennington described it, that one might use when offering a cup of tea to a visiting neighbor). Boo miraculously held his sit for the required three seconds, and there we were facing our nemesis.

"Boo, down," I said, giving my hand signal at the same time, my heart thumping so wildly that it was almost impossible to keep my cup-of-tea voice from quivering. Boo began to bring his front legs out in preparation for bringing his front end down—*yes!* I thought—but he stopped and got distracted by the volunteers who were waiting to pet him in case we actually got to the aptitude portion of the test. I'm sure he wondered why he couldn't just go see these nice, smiling people instead of having to lie down in the middle of this cold floor.

"Down," I said again, my hand signal a little more emphatic, but my voice still very much in the cup-of-tea tone. It's important to have this tone on a visit because we don't want to be barking commands at our dogs. It would be inappropriate for a variety of reasons from the client's point of view, and it could increase a dog's stress levels on a visit, which we never want to do. If we practice giving commands in a cup-of-tea tone of voice, our dogs learn to respond to calm, gentle commands. Boo looked away from me on the second command.

No, no, no! I thought.

As in baseball, we got three tries. "Down," I asked him again, hand signal quite emphatic yet cup-of-tea voice still in place, and I waited. The whole room was so quiet that I could almost hear the volunteers willing Boo to lie down.

Slowly, he started to pull his front feet out again, hesitated . . . and this time continued to pull them away from his body but just halfway. Then, he twisted his back end like he has to so he can fall over the rest of the way. *Boom!* He was down with a bit of a thud!

He had to stay there for a three count.

"One Mississippi," Kay said. No one, not one person, in that room breathed.

"Two Mississippi." *Please, Boo, oh, please!* I thought and wished.

"Three Mississippi!"

The room exploded in cheers of delight. I almost cried. But Boo and I still had over a dozen more exercises to go through in order to finish the evaluation, and I didn't want to celebrate prematurely. While I managed to keep Boo in place for "Stay" by constantly praising him, and he happily performed "Come" from the interaction with Diane, we still had the last exercise in the skills portion, "Reaction to the Neutral Dog," which is often the most difficult. Dogs' impulse to stop what they're doing and turn their attention to another dog who suddenly appears is very strong. In this exercise, two dogs have to ignore each other as their handlers stop to shake hands and then move on, but sometimes it almost seems as if the testing dog is like a person lost in the desert who finally sees another person and wants to call out for comfort but isn't allowed to. Imagine going for a walk with your child, passing another parent on the street with her child and stopping for a brief conversation without the children responding to each other at all! In short, this one is hard for a lot of dogs for a lot of reasons. Given Boo's affinity for other dogs, it was going to be hard for him, too, but he managed to keep his monkey-dog noises under control, and I managed to keep him close to my side as we passed the neutral dog.

Although we passed the skills portion of the test, Kay and Diane pulled me aside to talk to me before proceeding. As an evaluator myself, I know what Boo and I must have looked like: a scruffy and tousled team who could barely execute a simple down command. Kay and Diane were concerned that Boo would be overly stressed by the more demanding aptitude portion of the test. Most dogs who don't do well in the skills portion, who squeak by like Boo did, bomb out in the aptitude section. We scored 1s on almost all of the skills exercises. I assured them that Boo would be able to handle the aptitude section. "If I feel he's faltering," I said, "I'll stop the test myself." I'm sure it was only because Kay and Diane trusted me as an evaluator that they agreed to go on with the testing.

As expected, when the aptitude portion began, Boo was handled more and more vigorously. "Overall Exam," "Clumsy and Exuberant Petting" and "Restraining Hug" are the first three exercises of the aptitude portion, and a dog might encounter each of these on an everyday visit. Diane touched him everywhere, his feet, teeth, ears, underbelly and anywhere else she could think of, then made increasingly loud, crazy, bizarre noises while she petted him oddly before suddenly giving him a full body hug. I was right there next to him with my hand on his sternum (a calming pressure point), praising every good thing he did and telling him he was the best. When Diane had her hands on Boo, I did, too, supporting him and reminding him I was right there for him. Boo was doing fine with these.

Moving to "Staggering, Gesturing Individual," I realized that it was here that the difference between Dante and Boo would pay off for Boo. Whereas Dante woofed at this exercise once before when the volunteer actually growled at him, Boo just didn't care. In typical Boo fashion, he approached the gesturing individual gingerly and with just enough polite enthusiasm, as he had when he approached the little girls in the store. He was then subjected to the "Bumped from Behind" exercise and again didn't care. He didn't even look back, as many dogs do. He just moseyed on to the next set of people to greet the "Angry Yelling" volunteers who had just finished a loud, supposedly angry conversation. Boo didn't care that they had been yelling. He just wanted them to pet him now that they had finished their faux argument.

At last came the "Crowded Petting" exercise. Normally, when I teach classes in preparation for this test, I instruct handlers to always manage how many people pet their dog at once. With Dante, I never let more than one person pet him at a time so I could always know what was going on and be ready to get him out if necessary. Dante was goofy and had a typical wouldn't-hurt-a-fly mentality, but eighty-five to ninety pounds of startled dog can knock over things and people with ease. But for Boo, the crowded petting was his time to shine. I let everyone pet him at once; this was what he'd been waiting for. His body was tranquil, with a relaxed, slightly open mouth, happily panting as everyone cooed around him.

We completed the "Leave It" exercise as Boo ignored the toys on the floor, and I was left with the last hurdle, "Offered Treat." Boo often mistakes fingers for treats, and he needed to make the correct choice and not take Diane's finger. I instructed Diane to hold the treat in her flat hand like she would give a treat to a horse. She followed my instructions and walked away with all her fingers.

Boo passed.

Kay and Diane were stunned and really happy for us. Our scores were wacky—the opposite of a standard successful evaluation. Typically, a team will score 1s and 2s in the skills section, then we see a holding pattern, or the team drops to only 1s in the aptitude section. Boo did just the opposite of normal and still passed!

This is probably one of the greatest lessons Boo can give anyone whose life he touches: you don't have to be normal to find success. He had had the aptitude all along. It was just a matter of me helping him master his fears and the skills necessary for the test. Like all of us at one point or another, Boo just needed someone to stay faithful to him until he could succeed.

8
The Graduate

I'm often called in to consult for families who are having issues between their kids and their dogs. These can involve either miscommunication between children and their dog or actual aggressive behavior from the family dog.

I remember two little boys who loved their dog very much. I was called in to help with the dog's jumping and general manners. It wasn't until I started asking the boys what games they played with their dog that I found out the real reason I was there.

"We chase him in the yard, but then he chases us—"

Mom interjected, "Rex jumps on them."

The boys apparently felt a bit more bold: "He jumps real hard, and he bites us."

I asked the boys, "What do you do when he jumps on you?"

"We yell at him and push him off."

Mom said, "He's not really biting. He's just grabbing their clothing, and I heard they should knee him in the chest, but he's too quick, and they're too small."

"Is there anytime you guys have fun with him when he's not jumping or mouthing you?"

The boys shook their head sadly, as if worried they were going to get into trouble, as Mom said, "No, but they really love him."

"Is there any other time he jumps on you?" I asked. They really didn't have to answer that one. I pretty much knew the answer, but I wanted them to feel part of the process.

"When we come home from school."

The best approach in this situation was to establish a better communication system for the family to use with Rex, ask them to be sure they were rewarding only the wanted behaviors and managing or ignoring the unwanted while making Rex work for everything he wanted. Nothing, from attention to food, would be free for Rex anymore. We set up exercises and management strategies specifically for the boys that would allow them to spend positive time with their dog, empowering them and rebuilding their relationship with Rex. All the yelling and pushing created a dysfunctional relationship. The dog needed to play with them, and jumping and puppy mouthing was all he knew, so he put up with the things he didn't like—the yelling and kneeing. The boys, meanwhile, wanted to play with the dog they had begged their mom for, so they kept trying to play the only game they knew how to play even though they didn't like the jumping and occasional mouthing. Left unchecked, this could have resulted in an aggressive bite if the dog had gotten fed up.

(Consultations like this fall into a gray area where animal-assisted education and family behavioral consultations overlap. I often use the same strategies in each to allow the child to feel confident and empowered around the dog without using force or fear—leaving both dog and child at ease with each other while they are rebuilding a relationship that has been strained by a bite or a threat.)

The first exercise I did with the boys and Rex involved teaching him the go say hello command. This taught him to approach the boys with his head at their feet. For kids, this is great because the dog's snout is not right in their face. For the dog, it's great because there are yummy treats at the kids' feet. For the parents, it's great because this is one of the best remedies for jumping dogs. The boys and I then taught Rex the settle for reading command that we use on a reading visit, when children read books to dogs. Rex learned to just lie next to the boys for yummy snacks while they worked on their reading skills and rebuilt their trust in their dog.

"You're great at this!" said the boys' mother at one point during the consultation. "Do you have kids?"

My heart sank because I'd been asked this question on enough consultations to know what was coming after I said, "No, I don't."

"Oh, why not? You're so good with them. You'd be such a great mom!"

I took a breath and deflected the question with the usual jokes: "Dogs don't borrow the car keys, and you can't put kids in a crate."

Parents always laugh at those.

Those moments are always bitter, with a lingering pain that I've come to think of as emotional heartburn. Although letting go of the hope for children wasn't an easy thing to do, I was usually okay with it—except at moments like these.

Inspired by these sorts of consultations and the wise words of my friend and mentor Suz Brooks, who once said to me, "There are many ways to be a mother to someone," I started setting up school visits for Dante. They were a good opportunity to educate children about proper dog handling. One of our H.A.R.T. team leaders was Danielle Coletta, a third-grade teacher who was eager to bring visiting animals into her class-room. Incorporating the human–animal bond into education in the United States dates back to 1916, when the ASPCA first began formal humane education programs for school children in New York City. In 2002, eighty-six years later, this was still an uphill battle.

Danielle worked tirelessly to convince her principal and superintendent of schools that this program would not be a recipe for disaster. When the hurdle of permissions was cleared, Danielle and I put together a classroom-visiting plan that matched her curriculum. Our goal was to integrate humane education and just-for-fun learning, employing the dogs once a month throughout the year to support the various lessons she was teaching. When her class was working on volunteerism, we would talk about the dog's volunteer visits. When she was teaching her class about careers, we would talk about all the different kinds of careers that dogs can have. Danielle is a patient and caring teacher who understands that kids, like dogs, need to have fun when learning and that positive reinforcement works just as well for children as it does for pets. This understanding allowed her to use the visits to shape behaviors in her classroom. By behaving well in class, for example, children could move to the top of the list to pet the furry visitors. We were also able to use the canine-interaction skills we were teaching the children to explore important concepts: empathy for others, how to care for another person, accepting differences and working with individuals' strengths and weaknesses.

After all the work we did in preparation for Dante's first classroom visit, I was nervous when it came time for the visit itself. Almost immediately, Dante proved I'd had nothing to worry about. Sweeping the kids off their feet, he bounded in, flapping his three-foot tail in a happy-dog circle that caused waves of giggles, to cascade around the classroom as he magically transformed all the students into Dante lovers with his patented tongue-bandito greeting. This first lesson was a general introductory lesson about dogs. Danielle had had the kids read doggie books before the visit and planned to have them write doggie stories or draw doggie pictures afterward. I talked about caring for dogs, feeding and grooming them, where they like to be petted and so on. "They don't really like to be petted on the head," I said. "They usually prefer the neck by their ears." I then gave the kids the rules for the greeting process.

Then, we asked them to come up and pet Dante, who by now was trembling with excitement to see them. Each child had to go through three steps to greet the dog: First, ask the handler if you may pet a dog (dogs without handlers to be asked may not be petted). Second, if the handler says it is okay to pet the dog, hold out your hand gently so the dog can sniff it. Third, once the dog has had a sniff and shown gentle interest, you can pet him around the ears or the chin.

As the kids followed the steps, one by one, Dante sat politely, trying very hard to keep his jittering excitement under control, until each child had finished petting him. Then, with his pent-up exuberance, he uncoiled his overlong tongue and rewarded himself for being a good boy by licking each new buddy from chin to forehead. This elicited belly laughs from some, "Yuck!" from others and restrained smirks from the boys who wanted to look tough.

The first year, we didn't have Boo help us with the second visit of the fall semester, but once we did, he became a fixture as the second-visit dog, accompanied by another visiting-dog team, usually one of the release guide-dog Labs. Like Boo, many of these dogs had opted for a different career than the one for which they originally studied. They had all been slated to be service guide dogs for a person with visual impairment. For many release guide dogs, the career shift to visiting work is a natural choice.

Sometimes Boo came with the lovely Miss Waverly, a gentle, friendly vanilla Lab, or her mother Leeann, another gentle vanilla soul. (I like to call yellow Labs vanilla because I feel it shouldn't just be the brown ones who get to be associated with a yummy dessert treat.) Other times, Boo's partner would be Miss Olympia, Dante's favorite, easygoing black Lab, or Vesta, sweet and bouncier than some of the other girls. Boo was happy to be with any of these girly dogs, and they were all just lovely with him. Waverly and Leeann, who had both been breeding dogs and had several litters of puppies between them, seemed to take to Boo in a protective way, as if he were one of their pups. Vesta, who was closer to Boo's age, was his bouncy buddy. Miss Olympia usually looked at Boo as if to say, "You seem nice, but where's your big brother Dante?"

This second visit, the Boo visit, was really about two big lessons: illustrating clearly for the kids that we all have strengths and weaknesses as we learn and that if we persist, we can all achieve in spite of any limitations; and teaching them that individuals with disabilities are just like you and me. Danielle would prepare the kids by having them read books about dogs and/or people who had special needs or special skills.

We started the visit by asking the kids to identify any differences they saw between the visiting dogs.

"Boo is smaller," they would ring out in cacophonous chorus—they typically started with the obvious size differences—or, "Waverly is yellow." It was trickier with Olympia and Vesta, as they were black like Boo and closer to his weight, but a couple obviously detail-oriented kids would shout out, "Boo has white on his toes" or "Boo has white on his belly" or "Vesta has a longer tail."

Once we had the kids connecting with the dogs,

we started demonstrating training methods—verbal commands and hand signals to sit, down, stay and walk on a leash, as well as parlor tricks, if the dog knew them, like paw, crawl or bow—so the kids could see that dogs learned in much the same way they did. Just as teachers show children how to solve a math problem, for example, we show dogs what we need them to do by either luring or shaping. Then, just as children try doing something the teacher asks them to do, the dogs try a command. When they succeed, the kids get rewarded with a good grade or a gold star, while the dogs get a yummy treat. The kids gobbled up these demonstrations.

We had to describe the differences in how we lure and shape dogs because it's somewhat different from how we teach kids. When we lure dogs, we usually take a snack or toy and have the dogs follow that with their nose until their body is in the desired position (sit, down, etc.), then we praise and reward. Soon afterward, we attach the verbal command, and we are on our way to training a verbal command. When shaping, we simply wait for the dog to do something we like and then praise and reward it. The dog will do it more frequently to earn more rewards, and soon after we can jam our command in just before the dog goes into the routine, again putting us on our way to building a verbal command. Both are valuable in many ways. I prefer luring for quick, simple things like sits and downs, but I like shaping for complex things like tricks, and occasionally I will use both together.

Switching the kids' interest from training the behaviors to the dogs actually using those skills on visits, we would describe the types of visits the dogs make, the kinds of people they see and the things they need to know to do this work. When possible, we would bring some pictures of the dogs at work and at home living with their families (humans and animals). I had pictures of Boo as a baby wrestling with Dante, about ten times his size, and pictures of Boo snuggling on the couch with Merlin, the aloof gray cat, or doing some group begging with Atticus. The students gazed at the pictures, enchanted.

Once the kids finished devouring the pictures, we would ask them what they thought of these dogs. "We love them!" the kids always chorused.

The natural next question was, "What do you think the dogs' families or the people they visit feel about them?"

Again the kids would sing out, "They love them!" And they were right. These kids understood clearly what many adults miss—that these animals were loved like family members.

These questions had a purpose. Just like shaping any behavior, we were incrementally shaping how the kids would approach the real topic of the discussion, which we reached when I asked very slowly, to be sure they all heard me clearly, "What would you think if I told you Boo had some disabilities?"

Danielle has reported to me that she always loves this moment in the visits more than any other. We could almost hear the kids blinking as they sat silently, pondering the question. Before they could answer, we showed them Boo's disabilities by demonstrating the simple commands again, but this time asking the kids to watch carefully for the differences between the two dogs and their behaviors. When both dogs lay down at the same time, the kids could clearly see the difference between them. The Lab would pull herself downward to the floor effortlessly, fluidly, as if doing a long-practiced yoga exercise. Boo's difficulty was obvious in comparison, as he would struggle just to get his front legs out, strain to flop his back end over and finally fall clumsily onto the floor. The kids were mesmerized, watching closely as if they were trying to see the sleight of hand in a magic trick.

We demonstrated another behavior that clearly showed Boo's mobility difficulties: the paw parlor trick. Whichever Lab girl had come with us would gracefully lift a front paw and place it gently into her handler's waiting palm. Boo, in the meantime, struggled to pick up one front foot without falling over, and once he had done that, the best he could manage was to thrust his wobbling leg out like somebody might thrust a crutch or a cane out to point at something. If he got lucky, his paw might hit my waiting hand, but it was always a rough movement, as if he were swatting away a bug. It was comical, sad and inspiring. Boo tried so hard to do the requested parlor trick and seemed so happy and proud that he got sort of close to it. It made me think of the high-wire clowns who always look like they're about to fall when they're really in complete control—except Boo really always *was* just about to fall.

The kids were now primed for the big question: "Does this change how you feel about Boo?"

They proclaimed without pause, "No!"

"Is he just as nice, fun and lovable as the other dog?"

"Yes!"

"What about people?" we asked. "Do you think a person with disabilities might be just as nice, fun and lovable as a person without disabilities?" The kids' mental gears whirled as they pondered this, and we could discuss the idea that everyone has strengths and limitations just like Boo. This sparked a lively class discussion, and the third graders always concluded that we should all accept everyone's differences, limitations or disabilities unconditionally, just as they had accepted Boo unconditionally. It was an incredible joy to see Boo help kids decide to accept others without prejudice.

The joy had a personal dimension as well because, while my disabilities are mild compared with other folks', I know the sting of being stared at and judged. I could usually hide my dyslexia, but occasionally a job duty—composing an e-mail or drafting a press release—would expose my "condition," as some people euphemistically liked to call it.

My physical disabilities were more difficult to conceal, and my inability to do so meant I often found myself in situations that were beyond humiliating. Two times before I started using a cane and stopped riding the subway, I fell in a crowded rush-hour train car. It was a new kind of shame for me to lay in the middle of an early-morning mob of bleary-eyed, impatient New Yorkers, everyone just staring at me because I'd inconvenienced them—with not one offer of help. It made me realize just how much people with a disability are often viewed as an annoyance or an intrusion by "normal" people. Now, with Boo, I could show these kids another way to respond to differences and disabilities: with affection and acceptance. Maybe one day one of those kids would grow up to be the person on that crowded train car in the future who doesn't look with scorn on the fallen, humiliated woman and actually holds out a hand to help her get up and regain her dignity.

When we asked the kids to write stories and draw pictures of ways they planned to reach out to someone they knew who had special needs, we told them they could be a person or a dog who was offering help. Most of them chose to be a dog, and when they drew their pictures, they were often little black dogs with some white on their chests and paws. Although the effectiveness of dogs and other affiliative animals to help teach empathy, compassion, self-worth, nurturing and other positive human traits was obvious to us on these visits and has long been anecdotally accepted by individuals and families with pets, it's only in the last two decades that solid research has shown us how right so many pet owners have been over the years. Elizabeth Omerod, veterinary surgeon and chair of the Society for Companion Animal Studies in London, noted, "For many years, the valuable role of pets in children's development has been recognized. But recently, the positive health, educational and therapeutic benefits of having pets have been scientifically investigated and acknowledged. . . . Studies demonstrate that children who interact with animals have higher levels of self-esteem, greater empathy and better social skills."

In addition to providing training and testing for visiting teams like Boo, Dante and me, Pet Partners has been at the forefront of getting the word out about the many advantages there are for children who interact with pets. For instance, one Swedish study suggested that pet exposure during the first year of life is associated with a lower prevalence of allergic rhinitis and asthma in children ages seven to thirteen years old. Other assorted studies linked family ownership of a pet with high self-esteem and greater cognitive development in young children. Kids with pets at home score significantly higher on empathy and prosocial scales than those without pets do. Scientists know that when adults and children are under pressure, a number of stress hormones circulate through their entire systems, and while these hormones immediately affect mood, they can ultimately cause inflammation in cells throughout the body. We have also learned that petting our dogs, cats or other domesticated affiliative animals creates other neurochemicals that generate calm, happiness and a sense of well-being. Some therapy animals have been called furry Prozac. Sometimes I feel that pets are like duct tape: is there anything they can't do for us?

The fall I started the humane education program with Danielle's third-grade class, Mom and Dad

213

came up for a visit to see the leaves of the Northeast and spend some time with Lawrence and me for our early October birthdays. Our communication was more easygoing than it had ever been before. Mom and Dad enjoyed spending time with the dogs (and probably Lawrence and me, too). As Dad watched me working, I could tell he found my positive-reinforcement methods curious. He came from the old school of dog training, with heavy-handed punishment. At one point, Boo did something other than what I'd asked for, and Dad said, half jokingly, "In the old days, we'd just take a newspaper to that."

When I started explaining that my training choices were based on the positive-reinforcement quadrant of operant conditioning and that I wanted to avoid the fallout of punishment, I could almost see the wheels spinning in Dad's head. His degree in childhood education and psychology gave us a common ground of learning theories and the parallels between how all animals—two-footed and four-footed—learn and process information. He actually thought about what I had said, and I spied him later on praising Boo for leaving something on the floor alone instead of picking it up. Dad's recovery had removed his harsh, judgmental streak. I was shocked that I had a welcome, strangely settled feeling about my relationship with him after so many years.

I couldn't take Mom and Dad on one of the in-school visits, but luckily, their arrival coincided with the AATEA class, and I was able to bring them to one of our more lively sessions. This was the same class, with some tweaks, additions and subtractions, that I had been teaching since the early days with Dante—the class geared to prepare teams for their evaluation and teach them the skills they would need for the actual visiting.

Mom and Dad had no idea I would be putting them to work when they attended the class, but they got to play various roles as clients that the teams in training might meet on a visit. They were given faux limitations, such as a limp (since Dad had just had his knee replaced, he didn't need to fake that one), an inability to reach out with their arms, bad hearing or any number of other possibilities we could come up with to prepare the teams to be on their toes when visiting. Buried within Mom and Dad was a sense of mischief that had begun to shine in their retirement, so they were good at this exercise and thoroughly enjoyed the managed chaos of silly toys dancing all over the floor, balls bouncing everywhere and teams trying to keep their dogs focused on their visits.

Mom and Dad had such a blast in the class and on their trip in general, taking pictures of all the lovely colors of the leaves we had that season, that they spoke of it for years afterward. Although Dad and I had not spoken about the abuse since his suggestion that I go to Al-Anon meetings, we had spoken about recovery in general terms, and we knew we were walking parallel paths and had made pretty good progress on our individual quests for contentment. Mom had long ago dropped any involvement in any kind of recovery, but she still benefited from Dad's continuing work in AA. In spite of the fact that I was the world's greatest pessimist, I could honestly say that their trip up—along with all the positive communication that went with it—showed me that Mom, Dad and I had reached a turning point, a place of quiet calm. We were all pretty happy with that.

Boo, too, was happy as he continued to enjoy his visits with the kids in Danielle's classroom. The second time I brought him for the acceptance visit, none of the additional teams could make it. I had no idea how we were going to compare Boo with another dog, so instead I asked the kids to compare him with their recollection of Dante from the first visit of the semester. They remembered that Dante had lain at my side in a one-hip-over position (a hard-earned settle command), patiently waiting until he was cued to get up and greet, at which point he went from a casual, lounging dog to his more typical mister-happy-go-lucky tongue bandito, until I asked him to settle again for the wrap-up of the visit.

Boo, of course, was different. There were only a few places where he felt comfortable lying down for long durations, and the hard floor of the classroom wasn't one of them. During the presentation portion of his visits, he would usually be up and moving around, sniffing various things while staring happily and invitingly at the kids, panting his happy goofy pant. When it became clear to him that the kids weren't going to be saying hello right away, he would begin to sniff around my chair or behind me while I made boring "blah, blah, blah" human noises.

Boo's habit of continually moving in the same pattern could be very distracting to some of the other teams on visits, so when we had another dog with us, I usually had to give Boo a truckload of treats to keep him in a sit or a down. Since there were no other dogs on this visit, however, I let him do what he liked. He spent the introduction portion of the class exploring desks, pencil trays and the overhead projector, all while on leash. He only had six feet to range, but he found many things in that space. As always, as he explored, he occasionally bumped into things, and the kids giggled as if he were clowning around on purpose.

When we got to the part where I asked the students if they could see any differences between Boo and what they remembered of Dante, they said many of the things I had expected.

"Dante is much bigger," said a few of the kids.

"Dante is brown with black, and Boo is black and white," said another handful of kids.

"Dante is lazy," said one kid. Taken aback, I asked him why he thought that. "Because," he said, "Dante just laid there last time, but Boo is really busy."

I couldn't explain to the kids that Dante's "laziness" (that well-practiced settle command) was a huge achievement that had taken years of practicing and perfecting and that Boo would never be able to achieve these levels of cognitive success, but it didn't matter. What mattered was that the kids loved both dogs and thought it was great fun that Boo was busy investigating, sniffing around and occasionally bumping into things for their amusement.

My Little Boy Boo was sweet, soft, clueless, poor-sighted and clumsy, but when it came to tackling major life lessons, he was a master of deftness and poise.

9
Boo's Gift

Boo was never a dog to alert us to anything. Someone pulling into the driveway? Deer eating our roses? Someone at the front door? Dante and Atticus would sound the early warning barking system; beginning quite ferociously, they would quickly change their barking tune to "Oh, boy!" if it were someone coming for a visit. Boo would then follow them in the "Oh, boy!" barking, his head up in the air doing his coyote-howling-at-the-moon imitation, as he let out a "whoo, whoo, whoo" kind of bark. Playful and full of hope, it seemed to be Boo's way of saying, "Hey, guys, are we having company? I love company. Who is it, who is it? Yay, company!" I don't think it would have occurred to Boo to bark if we were being burgled or the house were on fire.

But there was one evening when Boo broke character and alerted us in a different way to a different kind of trouble. It was one of the worst nights of my life, but I will always be grateful to Boo for calling the alert.

A very snowy first weekend in December, a couple of friends and I attended a dog-training conference just outside Kingston, New York. The presenter, Turid Rugaas, a Norwegian dog trainer, is a well-regarded authority on canine body language. Turid was the first to begin discussions about dog body language and the emotions that go along with it. Her work became a cornerstone for many of us in the dog-training world because she illustrated that dogs as social animals use language to communicate with other members of their species for survival and cooperation. She also theorized that if dogs can try to diffuse an anxious situation within the social unit, that means they can *feel* anxious or stressed, and they care about the cooperative nature of a social society. Prior to Turid, this thinking was often frowned upon for being anthropomorphic. Her work was a wonderful eye-opener for many dog trainers and behaviorists and allowed us to understand what dogs actually meant by certain body language signals. We had to acknowledge that these animals were indeed communicating and, in doing so, accept that training a dog was a two-sided conversation. Turid observed that when dogs turn their heads, for example, they are likely averting their gaze in an attempt to diffuse their stress levels or tell you they are uncomfortable with the situation. When you call a dog to you and she moves slowly past another dog, she's not being disobedient or trying to dominate you through slow movement;

she's recognizing that she needs to show a kind of doggie politeness to the other dog.

Atticus, Dante and Boo stayed at home with Lawrence that weekend, snowbound. For many dogs, snow means "party!" and seems to ignite their joy and energy. Even older dogs like Atticus will often become nutty. At thirteen years old, the sixty-five pound Atticus was approximately eighty-two in human years. (To calculate this number, I didn't use the dog-years equation that ages dogs seven years for every one they live. As we have come to understand our dogs better, we've realized that the size of the dog determines the rate at which he ages. In short, a twenty-pound dog the same chronological age as Atticus, for example, would only be the equivalent of sixty-eight in human years.) During the first snow of each winter, he would run so fast that it seemed like his butt was going faster than his front end until it scooped under him as if to push the front end faster and faster. This year after a little romp in the snow and some zooming butt-scooping laps, Atticus began to have trouble trudging through the snowdrifts on his way into the house. Panting heavily, he fell in the snow at the bottom of the stairs to the deck and fell again once up on the deck. The second collapse, more powerful than the first, left him unable to stand. His whole body seemed to quake and struggle for every hard-earned breath through his increasingly heavy panting.

Lawrence picked him up, brought him inside and begged the gasping dog not to die. "Please don't die," he chanted. "Please don't die when she's away. Please don't you dare die without her here." Atticus complied, and over the rest of the weekend, he seemed to recover.

Dr. Cindy had gone to the conference with me and left her car at my house so we could carpool. After I described Atticus's episode to her, she said she'd give him a look when we got back to the house. Upon returning late Sunday evening, we witnessed Atticus's typically exuberant, happy dance of joy that I had come home. There was nothing about his demeanor or appearance to make her worry. I figured he had just been fatigued by his silly snow fun—clearly a little too much for a dog his age.

In hindsight, Lawrence and I both remember noticing changes in Atticus over the next week. He appeared a bit more stiff when walking, he tired more easily and his head tilted just a bit to one side, almost as if he had had a stroke. However, because it had only been three weeks since his annual checkup, and he was in good shape for a thirteen-year-old dog, with normal heartbeats and good breathing, we didn't confer or compare our separate observations. We each believed he was just going through normal aging.

Meanwhile, my life was a runaway train. I had

just finished writing the 501(c)(3) for H.A.R.T. Programs; was doing two or three Pet Partners visits per week, alternating between Dante and Boo; was still working at the literary agency while doing part-time dog training; and now, as soon as I got back from the conference, I had to deal with the imminent arrival of new windows and doors for the entire house. The Sunday after the conference, in more bad weather, the material arrived, and the installation men came at the crack of dawn the next morning. Where there had once been windows to hold back the cold, there were now huge holes, architecturally dramatic but not so good for insulation. I started burning the cardboard boxes the windows had come in to keep the house warm, and because the work took up so much room, I had to double up some of the living room dog pillows. I caught sight of Atticus relaxing in prime warming position next to the fire on an über-comfy, double-high pile of dog pillows and chuckled at the thought that he had grown to love the luxuries in life. The day had gone well, the dogs enjoyed the visitors and most of the bigger windows were in, with the doors on the agenda for the next day.

Tuesday was going to be frenzied: I had to be up for the early arrival of the installation men, pop out with Dante for a quick third-grade visit, return home to continue monitoring the installation, catch up on some office work and end the day by going out again to teach two classes. Days like this were pretty typical. I had gotten good at jamming actual paid regular work into the cracks between volunteer visiting and not-so-great-paying training. Because Monday left me no time to get Dante ready for his visit, I had to bathe him and do his nails that night.

It is always necessary to be sure a dog's nails are trimmed and smooth before a visit. Neither Dante nor Boo would dream of intentionally hurting anyone on a visit, but dogs' nails can be sharp, and without a good trimming ahead of time, a simple request for a paw from a student could result in a scratch. I use a Dremel rotary tool to trim the dogs' nails, and since I knew Boo would be visiting later in the week, and Atticus always needed a trim (as dogs get older, it's important to keep their nails short so long nails won't interfere with how they stand or put unwanted pressures on aging joints), every dog had his pedicure that night.

That Monday had been a pretty good day for the dogs—snuggled by the warm fire, fun with the dog-friendly installation men and the evening capped off with the super-high-value treats they received for their nail-trimming efforts. Lawrence and I clearly remember all three of them sitting in a row on the rug in the dining room, looking at us with wet eyes as if to ask, "We can do it again, right?"

As Atticus aged, he had grown less and less comfortable in the bed next to me, so I kept a pillow next to my side of the bed. That way, whether he was in bed or not, he could still be by my side. I guessed that his joints were a bit sore and that having more room to spread out allowed him to position himself differently depending on his level of pain. Atticus's favorite pillow was an old, faded, very regal brocade dog pillow that I had restuffed with a threadbare down comforter when the original stuffing had begun to wear thin. Atticus was among a very small group of dogs on this planet (I'm guessing) who actually had a doggie bed stuffed with down.

Tummies full of treats and nails rounded and smooth, we all climbed the stairs (Atticus more slowly than the others) to bed that Monday night, Atticus on his down bed right next to me, Dante at the foot of the bed and Boo snuggled between Lawrence and me for his poky-Boo/snug-a-Boo position. There, "nestled all snug in our beds," just as in "The Night Before Christmas," we drifted peacefully to sleep. . . . Until we heard a series of bumping noises coming from somewhere else in the house. At first, we stirred only a bit in our foggy, middle-of-the-night state of drowsy confusion, but then there was a larger clang, and we both jumped up—noticing as we did that Atticus wasn't on his pillow, Boo was nowhere to be seen and Dante had abandoned his post at the foot of the bed. Following the sound of continuous clanging and banging took us into Lawrence's office across the hallway from our bedroom.

It wasn't unusual for Boo to move off the bed in the middle of the night to find a bit more room for himself on one of the dog pillows scattered around the room. However, this night it seemed that when he'd gotten up, he'd made a wrong turn somewhere and wandered into Lawrence's office. This room was the catchall room, especially when there was a chaotic project going on in the house. Lawrence didn't seem to mind working around boxes or furniture that didn't belong to him, so given the window installation, there were a few extra things in his office that night.

Some of those extra things were our dogs. We found Boo struggling, stuck in the tripod legs of a telescope, trying in vain to move toward Atticus, who had embedded himself in a little cavern he had made between the tripod, the Christmas decorations trunk and the solid log wall behind him. Dante, meanwhile, was navigating the extra items with ease but also seemed to be headed for Atticus. Atticus's breathing was hard and shallow, sounding just like it had the day he collapsed in the snow. Making our way toward him, we saw spots all over the floor where he had lost control of his bowels and bladder—very unusual for the dog who usually

226

held both with great control for hours. He lifted his head as I approached, and I could see that his gums were pale and his tongue looked dry. I called to him to get up and climb out of the little hollow, but he couldn't move. I could see the pleading in his eyes. I didn't know whether he was pleading for me to leave him alone or to help him out.

Lawrence finally freed Boo from the tripod cage and escorted him and Dante out of the office while I dug Atticus out from his furniture cave and hoisted him up. I'm still not sure how I carried all sixty-five pounds of him back to the master bedroom, but when I'd put him on the bed in his old spot next to me, his breathing was still hard and short. I stroked his whole body gently while Boo and Dante approached him in turn and sniffed him in the same order: first they sniffed his breath, then his ears and last his hind end. After the final sniff, they both each stood still for a moment and then walked away to their respective spots, Dante at the foot of the bed and Boo up to Lawrence's and my pillows. I will never know exactly what was going on in their heads, but I would be willing to bet that they had both said their goodbyes.

I snuggled next to Atticus as I had for so many years. His breath was the very definition of putrid. I knew he was dying but couldn't express it out loud.

"We can't take him to Bedford," I said to Lawrence. "He doesn't know them. He would be miserable at a vet's he didn't know." It was 5:30 in the morning, and Cindy and Julie's office wouldn't be open until 8:30.

"You're right," said Lawrence. "We can't do that to him."

"So, we wait?"

Lawrence was quiet for a moment. "We wait."

Atticus still seemed uncomfortable, so I put him on his down bed, hoping he'd relax, maybe even sleep a little, until it was time to go. Lawrence and I couldn't sleep, so we lay back down to wait for dawn to take Atticus to the doctor. His hard, labored breathing was as regular as storm surf, and I started to drift in and out of awareness until I heard him sigh a deep sigh.

Lawrence sprang up like a coiled spring. "He's gone."

I shot up and was at Atticus's side in an instant. His eyes were fixed, and he didn't seem to be breathing anymore, but I wasn't sure. Frantically, I called Cindy. "Cindy, it's Lisa Edwards." I think Cindy said something, but I don't remember what she said before I continued, "I'm sorry for calling so early, but I think Atticus is dead."

There was a pause before she asked, "What happened?"

I described the episode for her and knew she

was thoughtfully considering the situation until I asked, "How can I be sure he's dead?"

She said, "The eyes. The eyes will always have a reflex response even if he's passed out."

I aimed my finger toward his closed eye and pointed at them—no response. I touched his eyelid—no response. When I described this to Cindy, she said, "I'm sorry, Lisa, but he's gone."

It was still only six o'clock in the morning. He never would have made it to the emergency hospital, and I was glad we hadn't tried to get him there. I couldn't have lived with myself if we'd turned the last half hour of his time with us into frenzied screeching along windy back roads in the middle of the night. Instead, we all had the chance to say goodbye, with Atticus in his favorite spot at my side. If Boo hadn't been the klutz Lawrence dubbed him as a puppy, we would have woken hours later only to find that Atticus had died alone in a pile of his own urine and feces. I can't imagine a greater gift of dignity than what Boo gave Atticus and us that night simply by being devoted and clumsy—and I'll always be grateful that Boo woke us up that night so we could be with Atticus at the end.

The trip to the animal hospital with Atticus's body in the back of the wagon was icy in every way imaginable. The weight of the cold just turning to bitter winter made the air hang heavily, and there was some sort of amorphous rainbow formation over the reservoir. It wasn't the typical arched shape of a rainbow but a shapeless specter that drifted over the water and appeared to move with us as we drove along. We thought of this as Atticus's passing into whatever life comes after this one, or perhaps it was his way of saying goodbye. As I thought of all the myths of rainbows as bridges that take warriors to the home of the gods or allow pets to reunite with their humans after all have died, I began to think about the life of the dog who, like his namesake, Atticus Finch, had been a wise, patient guide and protector for his family, and about the moments that best portrayed his true character.

There was the day when Dante was chasing a ball in the dog run in Washington Square Park, and another dog tried to take the ball from Dante by biting him, hard. Dante screamed, which is risky because a dog scream can begin a dogfight or bring other dogs into an existing fight. At the sound of Dante's cry, Atticus sprang from his spot next to Lawrence and landed in front of Dante. With his back to Dante and teeth bared to the rest of the dogs in the park, Atticus circled Dante, warning the biting dog and all the other dogs to stay away until Lawrence could get there and escort them both safely out of the park. Dante had puncture wounds through his tongue and lip as it was, and he could have been more badly injured if Atticus had not stopped the fight from escalating. When humans protect each other out of love like this, we call them heroes. Atticus was a hero that day. The episode always reminded me of the scene from *To Kill a Mockingbird* when Atticus Finch sets up a chair and reading lamp on the steps of the courthouse to stand alone against the mob set to hang Tom Robinson.

As I remembered all the wonderful things about Atticus, it became clear that the simple act of picking him up that fateful day had shaped me for the better—more than most of the people in my life. He protected me for so many years when I lived alone in the East Village, gave me the gift of recovery and unconditional love and brought me a husband, a loving second dog, a vocation at which I seemed to excel, and Boo.

It was with this last thought that it struck me like a bolt of lightning: without realizing it, we had named our third dog Boo, like another hero from *To Kill a Mockingbird*, Boo Radley. In the hours after Atticus's death, the strange connection between Atticus Finch and Boo Radley and my own Atticus and Boo took on a spooky resonance for me. Both Boos were misunderstood and often bullied, and Boo Radley quietly watched over Atticus's children, Jem and Scout, just as our Boo's calling was to work with and help children. And on that

Halloween night, when Mr. Ewell tried to murder Jem and Scout, Boo Radley stepped in and saved them. Although our Boo's arrival on Halloween hadn't literally saved our lives, it had given us countless gifts that we would never have otherwise had, including allowing Atticus to be with his family at the end so he could die with love and dignity.

To quote Crazy Horse, Atticus picked "a good day to die." Since I had a school visit with Dante in the morning, construction during the day and classes to teach at night, I was able to keep myself occupied so my mind could slowly absorb the depths of the sadness that might otherwise have overtaken me like a tsunami. I was constrained by my early family teachings never to display to the world the weakness of emotions, so I spent the day putting on a quiet show of calm, but when we were finally alone that night, Lawrence and I were soaked in the sadness. For the next few weeks, it was difficult for us to make it through the day without weeping uncontrollably at a sight, a sound, a smell that reminded us of Atticus.

It even seemed that the dogs were grieving. Dante and Boo would start to chase each other in play, and then, as if a penalty buzzer went off in their heads, they would suddenly stop and just go lie down. Other times, I would hear Boo pace around the house from room to room, starting downstairs and finishing in the master bedroom. I followed him one day to see what he was doing. As if he was searching for something, he started by sniffing the couch in my office, where Atticus slept during the day when I was home. Next was the living room, where he would check out the dog pillows, then the front door, where Atticus often held vigil. When Boo found nothing on the lower level, he went upstairs to the master bedroom to check out my side of the bed, where Atticus also slept sometimes. Finally, after sniffing the spot where Atticus had died, Boo circled the bed, ending with his paws up on the credenza behind the bed, where Atticus's collar lay, waiting for the day we could bring ourselves to remove it. Boo sniffed the collar intently, gave out a sigh and then went to lie down. There is no doubt in my mind that Dante and Boo missed Atticus as much as Lawrence and I did.

The universe is a very efficient place that continuously re-creates itself, turning matter into energy and energy back to matter time and time again. In short, it recycles itself, and we and all we know are simply the by-products of stellar waste. Somehow, as dying stars scatter themselves on the solar winds to be born again as flowers on a distant planet in the spiral of this unremarkable galaxy, I knew Atticus would move heaven and earth and stardust to find a way back to us. We just had to give him some time.

By March, we started searching, with the help of Dante and Boo, for puppies, hoping to find one who might be Atticus. Perhaps I underestimated Boo's effect on Lawrence because even though he had fought me on adopting Boo, he was fully on board when it came to this puppy search. He may grouse at the dogs, but he cried like a baby for days with me after Atticus passed. When I told him I had found a litter of three black Lab mixes that were being shipped up from the South to be fostered in Stamford, Connecticut, we put in our application. It was approved, and I awkwardly asked if my two adult dogs could meet the puppies to see who got along with them. I was happily surprised when the rescue group said yes; too often, puppies are not allowed to meet adult dogs they are destined to live with, and this creates the potential for a lifetime of troubles. To allow people to be sure their dogs will accept the puppy *they* want, a proof of vaccinations for the adult dogs and a nice leash walk for everyone will keep things safe and secure for all. Our meeting was a little more chaotic.

"The mother dog isn't great with other dogs," the foster mother told us, "so I've sent her upstairs. But if you go into the living room, I'll bring the three pups to meet you."

Two of the pups had zero interest in Lawrence or me. They zipped and zoomed around the living room, bouncing off everything, treating me and Lawrence as just two more objects in the obstacle course, no different from the sofa, the chairs and the dog crates. However, the one oversized boy—exactly what I had *not* wanted— approached me politely and sat himself calmly and cheerfully between my legs. Lawrence liked this one.

"I didn't really want another bigger boy dog," I said, pointing to the girl puppy with some white on her, like Boo. But she ignored us and had no desire to do anything but chase her brother around the room.

"Let's see what the boys think," said Lawrence, just as I had said to him three years earlier. (Turnabout is fair play.)

We brought Dante and Boo in from the car to see the puppies. The smaller puppies remained completely focused on each other, pausing only for a drive-by sniff at Dante and Boo, after which they went back to their racing, chasing and pouncing game. The bigger puppy, however, sauntered over and sat patiently as Dante sniffed him intensely up and down. Once covered in Dante scent, the big baby dog made his way over to Boo, and there he sat as Boo favorably poke-sniffed him—a little more irregularly since Boo's sniffing skills were a bit rough around the edges.

"He's the one," said Lawrence.

I was the one outvoted this time around. When we got home, and the new puppy curled up on the mat at the front door, Lawrence was quick to remind me that this had also been Atticus's vigil spot. This was a good sign that we had gotten the right dog, but I was completely convinced after we took the puppy out to pee. When the new front door was replaced after Atticus's death, the door was reversed at my request. Rather than opening awkwardly from left to right, where it obstructed the stairway, it now opened from right to left so there was always clear passage out the front door. When we headed back into the house after the pup's first official pee on the front lawn, he immediately went to the left side of the door and sat. Opening the door from the other side, I gestured to him to move to the right, but he seemed adamant that he should enter from the left side. My doubts were gone, and I knew we had the correct dog—smart, loyal and officially stubborn.

He required a fitting name as majestic as his predecessor's. Again, we were stymied until later that weekend when we were watching *The Man in the Iron Mask*. Gérard Depardieu played the role of Porthos, the honest, extraverted, wine-guzzling, womanizing, gluttonous musketeer. As I watched a scene in which Porthos sauntered to the barn to hang himself, buck naked but for his boots, the baby dog sauntered past me, and I noticed the naked butt scars his mother had given him during, as we were told, some exuberant cleaning. The puppy's butt was a dead ringer for Gérard Depardieu's, and baby dog became Porthos.

For Boo, Dante had been the caretaking, surrogate mamma, and with Porthos, it was Boo's turn to become the nanny. To this day, Porthos puts up with behavior from Boo that he would never tolerate from another dog. Watching Boo try to teach Porthos mouth-wrestling skills was like watching a parent try to teach a fifth grader how to use a computer. Yet, despite the fact that Boo was constantly outwitted in all the games he played with Porthos, he managed to teach Porthos a terrific soft mouth. Mouth wrestling can sometimes be mistaken for fighting, but it is actually play that teaches dogs how to control their mouths—the pressure, the positioning. It's like kids playing scales on the piano, and playful mouth wrestling usually includes some slow, languishing noises that are very different from fighting noises, which are louder and more staccato. Mouth wrestling also generally only occurs between dogs who know each other well and trust each other. Trust is critical because they have their mouths wide open and intertwined with each other's.

On occasion, the babysitting assignment was

more than Boo could handle, and when I found Porthos with Boo's back leg securely in his mouth, obviously testing the back-leg-bite/hold maneuver on Boo, I had to laugh. Our family was different, yet intact, once again.

10
The Little Dog Who Could Get His Wish

The humane education visits to Danielle's third-grade classroom were going so well that she and I talked about setting up a reading to dogs program. In 2002, this was a fairly novel idea in many libraries and schools. The now-standard R.E.A.D. (Reading Education Assistance Dogs) organization, run through Intermountain Therapy Animals, was only three years old, and few people knew about the benefits of the program. Danielle and I set up a couple meetings at the Mahopac library, but a presentation was difficult to create because there wasn't a lot of hard scientific data at the time.

We met with Joan Rose, the head of Youth Services, and another woman from the library administration and started by explaining what the dogs were doing for the kids in Danielle's classroom: building focus and helping them understand complicated vocabulary and concepts. The dogs made these new words and topics more interesting, less daunting and therefore generally more accessible for the kids. From there, we dove into the successes of R.E.A.D. An animal lover and an all-around sweetheart, Joan was very supportive, but her companion was unenthusiastic about the prospect of bringing dirty, "allergy-making" dogs into the new library building. And those were only her first objections.

"I don't get it," she said, her brow wrinkled in disapproval. "How exactly do the dogs help the kids read? It's not like they can help the kids sound out the words, is it?"

Danielle, Joan and I deflated like Thanksgiving balloons after the parade, and I struggled not to sarcastically answer, "Only if they're reading about woof repairs." Instead, I laughed my best cocktail-party laugh and said, "Of course not. We know from study after study that the mere presence of an animal lowers blood pressure and reduces tension. We also know that kids who are having trouble reading are often very stressed by even the prospect of reading."

"I still don't see how this is going to make kids want to read."

Stammering just a bit by now, I responded, "I know what it is to have difficulty reading. I'm dyslexic and was in remedial reading most of my early years." Restricting my dialogue to only those thoughts that would hopefully make our case, I was flooded with my internal dialogue. I hated to read and would avoid it like the plague, especially if an adult was standing over me, waiting to correct each and every mistake as if I were making them on purpose. A montage ran through my head of all the angry teachers who towered over me and said, "Just sound it out," as if I could actually put the letters together in a logical fashion when they were bouncing around on the page and masquerading as one another. Mom and Dad and I were instructed to endure the nightly book death march, when they would read a book to me and then have me read it back to them. I just memorized the text and then recited it back to them. I dreaded that every night. I know a dog would have been a much better reading companion for me in those days.

Turning away from my internal dialogue, I refocused on making our case for the reading program. "Dogs simply can't judge a child as she reads."

Silence.

"Without judgment," I continued desperately, "reading becomes fun. The more fun it is, the more kids will do it. The more they do it, the better they'll read." It all made such sense to me, and this woman didn't understand it at all. I felt like I was talking to someone who would have refused to believe me if I said the sky was blue.

I was one of those kids pulled out of class for brief but embarrassing "special" education a couple times a week. Whatever help it may have offered was immediately more than undone by the embarrassment, and instead of fixing my reading problem, it simply taught me how to hide it. When I was called on to read aloud in class, I would make a theatrical display of it all. Dramatic pauses in the right places, and no one would know I couldn't read the next word and was really stalling as I struggled to figure it out from the context.

I was so embarrassed and afraid to ask for help that I just jammed my homework into my desk in the hope that no one would notice. But when they did notice, the ultimate teaching tool of the day was applied: humiliation. I was forced to complete all my hoarded assignments in front of the rest of the class while they got to play and dance around for a holiday party. Thinking I was done with the shame, I was told I could only participate in the holiday dance if I played the role of the boy. With that last indignity, I learned to hate school and reading forever. (As if in direct retaliation to that, all my students graduate from my dog-training classes because they have tried and will all learn at their own pace just as both Boo and I did. It's my job to see that they don't have to do it on their own.)

Because of these personal experiences, I felt particularly passionate about the R.E.A.D. program. I just knew it could help a child who was struggling to read and feeling humiliated. Like so many with a learning disability, I was mistakenly considered lazy and in need of more punishment, more homework or more spelling exercises. I had spent most of my days in school (and too much of the rest of my life) believing I was stupid as a result. It all made sense later, after I was diagnosed with dyslexia, but the shame never washed away completely. That was why I was here in the Mahopac library, determined to offer a better way for kids who were afraid to read.

I was bombing. The woman in front of me looked like she hated my guts and obviously wasn't interested in anything I was saying. Finally, Danielle stepped in. "The goal of this program isn't to teach reading," she said, "but to encourage it, make it fun and make it a habit for the children's lifetimes."

The administration lady softened. I wasn't sure what Danielle said that I hadn't, but if it worked, I was happy for her to take over. "Part of what I, as a teacher, will be looking for here," Danielle continued, "is practice and fluency." Reading with fluency means having the ability to read connected text quickly, smoothly and without effort, with little conscious attention paid to the technical processing of the words. Fluency was something I had never learned as a kid and don't have a whole lot of even now. Danielle's explanation finally rang a bell for our unsupportive executive, her defenses began to lower and the discussion turned to logistics.

Since our meeting, many people have taken the time to research and document the practical impact of kids reading to dogs. In 2010, researchers from the UC Davis School of Veterinary Medicine found that when kids read to a dog once a week for ten weeks, their reading fluency improved anywhere from twelve percent to a whopping thirty percent. "I feel relaxed when I am reading to a dog because I'm having fun," one child told researchers. "The dogs don't care if you read really, really bad, so you just keep going," said another.

In another study at Johns Hopkins University, kids were asked to read aloud while hooked to blood-pressure monitors. As soon as they started reading, said researcher James Lynch,

> their blood pressure would instantly go up. Then, when we simply put a dog in to wander around the room, the blood pressure quickly lowered. What the animal did was take the child's attention away from performance anxiety or other fears that make academic performance more difficult.

These findings have helped inspire hundreds of Reading to Rover programs all over the country.

Petting a dog doesn't just lower blood pressure and stress, according to a study by University of

Missouri–Columbia researcher Rebecca Johnson, it also raises the production of mood-elevating hormones. Johnson drew blood samples from volunteers before and after they played with either a live animal or a robot dog. Levels of serotonin, a brain chemical that combats depression, surged in those who interacted with the live animal but not in those who interacted with the robot dog. "We also saw rises in prolactin and oxytocin," Johnson reported, "more of those 'feel-good' hormones." In short, research has confirmed that interacting with dogs bathes the brain in a happy soup of neurochemicals and hormones that increase kids' chances for successful learning and accomplishing challenging tasks.

Even before we had the benefit of these studies, Danielle, Joan and I believed a reading program would have a positive benefit for the kids, so we put our heads together to set up a visit that would best suit the H.A.R.T. teams and the library, and it is still run the same way ten years later. Following H.A.R.T. guidelines to keep visits to an hour, and limited by the size of the room to two dogs, we arranged the visit to accommodate eight children. Four children would read to each dog, one at a time, for fifteen minutes; this kept the dogs from tiring out and allowed the maximum number of kids to read for a reasonable amount of time. We began the program ARF (Animal Reading Friends) for kids with reading issues, but we ultimately included any child who wanted to read to the dogs.

Although I suspected Boo wasn't going to be the perfect reading dog, I knew I had to let him try. The ideal reading dog is able to relax and focus on the child without being overly energized or falling asleep. It's also helpful for a handler to teach a dog to "look at the pictures," either automatically whenever a book is held out or on cue when given a hand signal or verbal command. This proved tricky for Boo, but he found his own way to attempt it. When I started shaping the auto-picture-look for Boo, he got to the point where he would try to place his nose in the books, but his clumsiness and inexplicable eyesight often led him to bump into the books instead, knocking them around, stepping on them or standing on them directly, all while he tried in vain to figure out where the book and these (so-called) pictures were. It was a good laugh for all, but I quickly shifted gears to simply luring him so he only stuck his nose in to "see" the pictures when I led him in with a treat. Although that worked much better, I was concerned the library would begin to wonder why all their books smelled like liver.

Other really nice skills for a reading dog are a paw touch and a chin command. The paw touch allows the handler to ask the dog to touch something with a paw. This way, when children bring multiple books, they can ask the dog to choose one. Handlers can invisibly cue the dog to point to a book, but to the child, it looks like the dog has just picked the book she wants to hear. I tried this for a little while with Boo, but with his clumsy gait and the way he swatted repeatedly and awkwardly in random directions, I worried that he was going to rip up some of the books. In the interest of preventing library property damage, if kids Boo was visiting brought multiple books, I told them they could choose because Boo would be happy with whatever they liked.

The chin command allows handlers to ask a dog to place his chin on any surface and hold it there. If everyone is sitting on the floor, for example, the dog can place his chin on the child's leg, the handler's leg or a small pillow. The result is an unbelievably sweet pose that makes it look like the dog is staring intently and adoringly at the kids as they read. Boo could get into the chin position, but he simply couldn't sustain it for any duration, so I stopped trying to make him.

Boo was about as far from the definition of a perfect reading dog as it was possible to get and still be a dog. He had two operating modes only: up and about, and sleeping. Relaxation is not in his skill set. When he was around kids, he'd either be up and sniffing them or eagerly waiting for petting, smiling at them through his happy pant. He would never settle down around them for more than a few seconds at a time, and getting him to do even this took a truckload of treats—but only those few treats that were better than interacting with the kids. It was made clear to me over and over again, as I attempted to shape Boo into a well-trained, trick-doing, smarty-pants dog like Dante, that really the only way to visit with Boo was to allow his free spirit to guide the interactions while maintaining a reasonable level of control through the meager skills at his disposal. There were times when that seemed to work beautifully, and then there were times when Boo's free spirit got ideas that left me stymied, with no recourse but to try to hide my giggling.

Early in Boo's ARF career, he met a little girl with pigtails who was reading her book with lightning speed, almost as if Boo weren't there. Perhaps he felt the need to be acknowledged, or perhaps he was just being Boo, but he got up from his settle position and began sniffing her ears (he loves ears). Unfazed, the pigtailed little girl continued her blitz-reading. In response, Boo began to draw his nose up to those little balls of plastic pinkness that she was wearing to hold each pigtail high up on her head, but she kept the flow of the story going (good fluency, Danielle would say), so Boo increased the intensity of his investigation of the two petite, pink baubles closest to him. Because our intrepid speed reader didn't seem daunted by his clumsy nose-bumping on the top of her head, and because I didn't want to interrupt her, I simply watched as Boo gently sniffed and poked the tiny pink orbs. Then, in a slow-motion moment in which I seemed unable to move, he turned his head to one side, opened his mouth just wide enough to place one of the pink spheres between his molars, and began to gnaw on it as if to test it for its flavor or funness factor. At last, the girl paused her reading, but only briefly, as her eyes moved up to the corners of their sockets, straining to see what exactly that sound could be on top of her head. Recognizing that it was Boo trying to consume her pigtail holders, she shrugged and returned to her speed-reading, and Boo happily continued his gnawing for a few more seconds before I redirected him back to the settle. We were later told that the little girl said she'd had a lovely time in spite of the teeth marks on her pigtail holders.

Over time, Danielle began to notice that Boo had a knack for disrupting the reading process in the most needed places: when kids would get stuck and begin struggling. Time after time, she realized that his clowning around—poking at the book with his paw or snuzzling (the name I've given to Boo's unique combination of sniffing and nuzzling) the kids for attention—occurred when the kids were having trouble with a phrase or word. (Perhaps the pigtailed speed-reader was reading so quickly because she was nervous, and Boo was just trying to calm her down or maybe adjusting her speed by turning down one of the knobs on top of her head.)

One of the most dramatic fidgety moments for Boo came with a child who either just couldn't read at all or was so stressed by the situation that each word on the page fought with him. Simple words, such as *blue, up* and *the,* stymied this little boy. Whenever this happened, Boo would get in the child's face, snuzzling and bumping the book. Boo pawed at the book repeatedly, and all the while I struggled to get him into a settle. He'd follow the treat into the settle then bounce right back up and start the fidgeting again. Danielle noticed the difficulties the child was having. It was painful to watch, and his struggle against words, while valiant, wasn't teaching him anything positive. Danielle had a picture book in her bag of tricks with no words, and she asked the child if he'd like a different book. He was happy for the swap and began telling Boo the story he saw in the pictures. The little boy settled down to his picture book, Boo settled down at last to listen, and I, knowing just how hard the world is when words are the enemy, took solace in knowing that Boo had given this child a happy reading moment.

We're not sure what enables dogs like Boo to sense anxiety like this. Is it some undetectable scent or emotional microexpression? A 2008 study from the University of Lincoln in the United Kingdom reported that dogs have evolved face-reading skills to check for subtle signs of our moods. Unique among animals, dogs consistently exhibit left gaze bias when viewing human faces. It suggests that they have learned our faces are lopsided when we exhibit emotions. Because our left hemisphere governs the right side of our faces and plays a much greater role in determining mood, the right side of our faces reveals more clearly how we feel than the left side does. Dogs have learned to gaze to their left sides to better see our right sides, and by quickly checking the emotional side of our faces, they can tell whether we're happy, sad or angry, and react accordingly.

Given Boo's visual limitations, I wouldn't be surprised if he were incapable of the face-reading done by other dogs. Yet, there could have been other ways he knew the kids were struggling, like a shift in their voices or something yet unknown. There's no way to know what inspired Boo to interrupt struggling readers at just the right moments, but we know that he gave them all a perfect break from a difficult passage or word whenever needed. Taking a moment to pet him and help me get him back into a settle allowed the kids to shift gears from being stressed over a word or paragraph to laughing at Boo. In terms of brain chemistry, this allowed them to lower their stress hormones enough to get them back to a level where learning was not inhibited but actually supported by those feel-good hormones. What Boo was doing fell on the cutting edge of our understanding of neurology and brain chemistry, but for him it was merely instinct.

"Boo isn't the cutest dog in the program," said Joan Rose once, "but he's one of the most popular. He makes hesitant readers feel comfortable by clowning around, and he looks like he's listening to every word."

While the chewing of the pigtail holders is the best ARF anecdote for a good chuckle, my personal favorite is Erich's story. Eight years old when he started in the ARF program, Erich would grow so upset and discouraged by the mistakes he made when reading that he'd end up close to tears, the librarian told us.

"He feels the pressure is on," explained his mom, Maureen. "He *hates* to read aloud."

As Erich approached Boo's reading mat for the first time, Boo, ready to work his miracle for the night, knew instinctively what to do to make those feel-good hormones flow. Sniffing Erich's shoes first, which made him giggle, Boo then tickled Erich's ears with a wet nose and whiskers, and the little boy was laughing. By the time Erich pulled out a Franklin the Turtle book and began reading aloud, all his tension dissolved. Boo was super clownish that night, offering the little boy countless ear snuzzles, his doggie nose jammed time after time into Erich's book to "look at the pictures." The fifteen minutes that Erich had to read his story whizzed by, and when his time was up, he looked shocked that he'd forgotten to be anxious while reading to his new furry tutor. The only problem, as far as he was concerned, was that he hadn't gotten all the way through the book, and Boo had to leave the library without hearing the end of the story.

When Boo and I arrived for our next visit, Joan rushed over to us in such a great whoosh of excitement that I figured something was wrong. Then, she started telling me about Erich. She said, "This sweet little boy has come back again and again looking for Boo. He thinks Boo needs to hear the end of the Franklin the Turtle story."

Erich had come to every reading visit the library had for the last two months, in fact, always clutching the unfinished book and asking Joan whether Boo was there that night. Every time, when the answer turned out to be no, Erich would sorrowfully put Franklin the Turtle away and find another book to read to the dog who wasn't Boo. On this day, however, as soon as Erich entered and saw Boo, he headed straight for the familiar mat that said "Boo" all over it in brightly colored paint, stood waiting for Boo to complete his dance of greeting, starting with a shoe sniff, then an ear tickle and finally the face snuzzle. At the close of the snuzzle, Erich carefully removed a frayed bookmark from the book and resumed reading Franklin's story to Boo in the exact place where he'd left off months ago. Boo, for his part, resumed his clowning right where he left off. Erich visited a few more times with Boo in order to finish the story—Franklin was a very active turtle—but now we made sure each time we left that Erich knew when Boo would be there again.

"Boo would put his nose on the book," Erich said when the librarian asked how he knew Boo needed to hear the story, "like he wanted to know what happened next."

Boo wasn't the only dog who helped kids. Dante had fun while visiting, an entertaining goofball who made the kids laugh and relax through whatever disabilities they had. But Boo seemed to reach people on a much deeper level, bringing quiet changes that would last a lifetime. I was amazed by his ability to be generous given how little he really had when compared with more functional dogs.

Word of the lovely job the ARF dogs were doing at the library spread, and a manufacturer of doggie ice cream offered to set up an ice cream social for the dogs and the kids at the end of the spring semester (with doggie ice cream for the dogs and kid ice cream for the kids). It was a fantastic event but also a chaotic one. With over a hundred kids, parents, library staff and ice cream folks, the room was extremely congested and loud. Orphaned balloons floated through the air, and ARF certificates littered the floor. Several of the dogs there had some trouble, as dogs often do in circumstances like these. Their instinct to watch everything going on around them made the crowd very stressful, and their sensitive hearing was overwhelmed by the noise. Several simply shut down, unable to work the room. One threw up her doggie ice cream; of course, it could be, as Gramma J used to say, that she'd just eaten it too fast, but I suspect her little doggie insides were no match for the stress of the occasion. Boo, however, sauntered from child to child, sniffing toes, licking fingers, his stubby, malformed tail wagging wildly as he worked the room more enthusiastically than a politician at a fundraiser.

One of the other handlers came up to me, looking at Boo and shaking her head. "In the face of distractions," she said, "Boo just don't care."

He could be just as unflappable in a room with over a hundred strangers and delicious ice cream as he was in front of a video camera or working up close with a client who had spastic movements and loud vocalizations, as I would later see on his SPARC (Special Program and Resource Connection) visits with a girl named Ena. As much as I would have liked to take the credit for this, it was Boo's sensory deficits that made this gathering okay for him. Without great hearing and great eyesight, he didn't experience these crowds the same way other, normal dogs did. The converse is also true: the handlers of the dogs who were having difficulties could not fault themselves or the dogs. The ice cream social was a big challenge for the doggie guests.

Lawrence came to the ice cream social, too. Watching him that night interacting with Boo, telling him, like a proud papa, how pleased he was with him, I was struck by the changes in Lawrence's relationship with the clumsy pup and with all the dogs in general. Lawrence was more patient with them than he used to be.

He had always insisted that the way to train dogs was to be firm, loud and harsh with commands and corrections, but he watched as each dog worked more easily and more happily for me as I used calm, quiet, gentle commands that earned rewards when complied with and only time-outs or a loss of privilege as punishments when disobeyed. Without realizing it, Lawrence was becoming more positive and easygoing with the dogs. He was starting to listen to himself when he spoke to them, and always in the back of my mind was the question of how this would apply to children if we ever had any. It was a mixed blessing: good in that this was good parenting, bad in that Lawrence still would not discuss the possibility.

In addition to the library visits, I expanded Boo's career to include visits to Blythedale Children's Hospital in Westchester County. The long drive to Blythedale exacerbated the hip pain that had recently joined my personal parade of joint pains, but Boo needed kids, so I made every effort to get him to all the kid visits I could, no matter how hard the trip.

Blythedale Children's Hospital is a leader in the pediatric field, treating kids from all over the country with complex, often disabling medical conditions. Caregivers are forbidden by law to tell visiting teams what ails a particular child, but they can let us know about his or her specific needs and limitations. On one of Boo's first trips to Blythedale, we visited a little girl who was wheeled into the visiting room lying facedown on a gurney. The therapist told me the girl couldn't move much at all, but they hoped she might reach her hand out to pet a dog. Normally, having a client reach out to pet a dog is a fairly simple act, but given that this little girl's range of motion was about three to six inches, this was going to be tricky. The one hand that had some mobility was folded up near her chin with her arm tucked under her shoulder. For her to be able to reach out to pet a dog, the dog would have to be directly in her face, almost nose to nose with her. Pondering how to accomplish this, I pulled a chair up next to the gurney and put Boo in what I think of as his bug-a-Boo position.

One of the sillier things Boo does is sit on my lap like a child, literally. His butt sits on my lap with his body upright, belly open to the world and all his legs sticking straight out like a bug's. Because of his neurological issues, he can't relax his legs—this is what creates poky-Boo when he sleeps between Lawrence and me—so when he's sitting on my lap like this, his legs always stick straight out in a goofy way. He looks like a peaceful, happy, strange combination of bug, dog and child. It always makes everybody giggle, kids and adults.

When I put Boo into the bug-a-Boo sit by the gurney, I hoped it would motivate this little girl to pet him. It certainly got her attention, but he wasn't close enough for her to try to reach him. I tried leaning him over toward the gurney, and he rested his head on the edge of the bed about three inches from the little girl's face. She beamed at him, and he grinned at her, his mouth open, panting his happy pant, gently wooing her. As if she were breaking through stone, she moved her hand in tiny increments until she reached the side of his face. He moved just a bit more in her direction, and she was able to scratch him gently in the perfect side-of-the-face/lower-chin spot. I felt Boo's body sigh and saw the little girl's do the same. He remained in his awkward position for several minutes as the girl continued to bury her hand in his thick, soft fur, beaming as if she'd just received a wonderful new toy. The therapist was thrilled with the little girl's movements, the little girl was thrilled with the visit from Boo, Boo was thrilled with snuzzling this little girl and I was trying not to cry. Dante, for all his smarts, friendly nature and good intentions, could never have done this. Even if I could have balanced eighty-five pounds of Dante on my lap, he just didn't have Boo's Zen-like nature or his ability to snuzzle. Probably because of his poor vision, Boo may not really know just how close he is to people when he is sniffing them, so he ends up gently bumping into them with his nose midsniff.

On the long drive home after that visit, I was haunted and happy as I thought about the difference between what kids go through in hospitals now and what I went through as a four-year-old in traction for almost two months after breaking my leg, shortly after Gramma J moved in with us. The whole episode quickly became operatic defiance and crayon eating. I remember they tried to serve me something slimy and stinky one night, which turned out to be liver. I absolutely refused to eat it, so I was punished: no dinner and no TV. Alone in the room, hungry with no one to speak to and no TV to watch, I just made up stories and talked to the stuffed animals Gramma J brought me. They kept serving me liver, and I kept refusing to eat it. When the hunger got to be too much, I rummaged in the drawer next to the bed for any leftover candy. Sometimes I got lucky, but mostly I just had to eat crayons.

Each day was another battle of wills in the epic war I waged with the head nurse, a large woman dressed in the old-style, quintessential white nurse's outfit, complete with silly hat. When she walked, you could hear the strange sound that comes from the brushing of slip against girdle. She could have played fullback for any football team. Her frustration with my eating habits was the talk of the floor: I wouldn't eat anything because it was all yucky. One day, she threatened me with "something horrible" if I didn't eat my soft-boiled egg. *I'm already tied to the bed,* I thought, *with weights hanging off my broken leg, no roommate, TV privileges constantly revoked and very few visitors. What more can she really do to me?* I made the typical four-year-old pouty face, folded my arms and stuck out my tongue as she left the room after the soft-boiled-egg gauntlet was laid down.

"You should really eat the egg," said the candy striper gently, trying to be helpful. "Then, she wouldn't be so upset."

"No," I said in my expansive four-year-old's vocabulary.

"Maybe it won't be so bad."

"No."

We went back and forth like this for a while until she realized that I wasn't going to fold, and she offered a compromise. "If you eat the toast and fruit, I'll flush the rest of the egg in the toilet."

I considered this for a few moments and accepted her compromise.

When the fullback nurse returned, she was pleased to see the meal consumed, but as she started to congratulate me on my compliance (and scold me further, telling me to be a better little girl going forward), she stopped.

"I see you ate *all* your egg," she said coldly. "Even the shell."

I looked her straight in the eye and said, "You told me to eat everything." She stormed out, her slip swishing angrily against her girdle.

Her threats and punishments taught me exactly

what science predicts: I didn't learn to eat the egg and enjoy it, I learned how to avoid the punishment and that she was not and would never be trustable.

I know what it is to be alone, unable to move and in pain, I thought as I got out of the car at home. Perhaps I didn't know this to the extent that the little girl on that gurney knew it, but I recognized the feeling nonetheless. The things that had gone wrong in my life were different from the things that had gone wrong in hers, but neither of us could—none of us can—go back to change them. We can, however, fix the past in our heads by making the present better, whether for ourselves or someone else. Boo let me do that on this day, and yet again I was reminded of the Boo lesson that we all have a niche—we just need to find it. It was as if on that day, when he pulled me to snuggle with the two little girls in the dog food aisle, he had said, "I'm going into the chrysalis now. Please let me know when I can fly with the children." And now that he had his little butterfly wings, they were starting to carry him to wonderful places.

Meanwhile, my time at the literary agency was drawing to a close. In addition to my waning interest in publishing, the office was whittling itself into a more streamlined organization, running very smoothly without much from me.

My boss and I made an exit plan for me to be out by the end of the year, consulting for a few months before cutting the cord entirely. To me, the signs were clear: I was meant to become a full-time dog trainer. Along with my experience and my multiple certifications, I would now have the time to devote to building a dog-training business of my own.

Just because I now had the time and experience to be a full-time trainer didn't mean everything would work out. I was taking a giant leap off a scary precipice into the unknown. It was frightening: how would I make ends meet? Teaching four to six classes a week in a retail environment wasn't enough to pay the bills. I needed to figure out how to teach more classes on my own and do more private consultations. Thankfully, all I did was put myself out there, and those two needs, inexplicably, managed themselves. Before I knew it, my calendar was filling up with private clients faster than I could keep track, and I had multiple locations to run my own classes.

This was a blessing and a curse, however, because once I set my life up to run like this, I had to live it, whether it was comfortable for me or not. I was the girl who, when called on to stand in front of my high school speech class for the first time, just ran out into the hall, unable to face the idea of speaking in front of everyone.

"When we first got married," Lawrence said, "if anyone had come to you and said that in six years you would be running your own business, regularly standing in front of crowds of strangers, speaking confidently and intelligently about dogs, you would have laughed in their face."

He was right. But like Boo, I had unique, isolated, savant-like qualities embedded in my general limitations, and in a way, I too was a butterfly breaking out of a cocoon to soar with my own wings—sometimes weak and rarely ideal, but always uniquely mine.

Although I was still mostly shy in general, when the topic was dogs, things were different. Then I could talk anywhere anytime. As a result, my general inhibitions slowly began to fade as my wings grew stronger. Atticus pulled me out of the hole where my recovery was stuck, Dante guided me to dog training and now Boo gave me that final push of confidence to go out there on my own. My first evaluator and mentor, Liz, once remarked on how mismatched Dante and I were in our natures. At that time, I was the shy, demure wallflower who spoke quietly in the face of Dante's big, gregarious, devil-may-care, fly-through-the-room nature. It was funny to realize that *I* was now the gregarious, demonstrative one flying through the room when I taught training classes.

I had to believe that Boo's butterfly wings would carry him just as far.

Seeing how Boo shone in his visits, one of our H.A.R.T. volunteers, who was a social worker at another school, asked us to set up visits to a class of first and second graders with learning disabilities who had trouble following directions and communicating directly, quietly and calmly. Once the kids met Boo and all the other dogs, they were very motivated to focus on the dogs. With the promise of a walk or a game of kickball with Boo and his canine visiting companions, we could get the children to quiet down and pay attention. It was as if he were holding court when the kids would approach for their petting. Because of the small size of the class and the need to direct cooperative play between the kids, two would often approach each dog at once and be required to take turns petting the dogs—not normally the ideal setup for a visit, but with Boo, of course, it was no problem. It struck me in this class that Boo was probably getting as much therapy as the kids were. Normally a pacer, he would frequently display repetitive, nervous behaviors, much like children on the autism spectrum. He would pace around and around, for example, without the appearance of really going anywhere. But this all ended when he was in face-to-face interactions with a child.

One of the games we played in this class was a version of Red Rover, but in our case, it was Red Rover, Red Rover, Let Waverly or Boo Come Over. The kids were split into teams, and each team had a dog. The dogs were across the room from the kids, and the kids were to call the dogs to them on cue. Because of the special needs of the kids in this class, it often took some time to get them organized enough to simultaneously call the dogs. While the kids were getting ready, Boo would fidget and pace while the other visiting dog usually sat politely waiting for her cue (reminding me of his early puppy class and the über puppies), but when the kids called him, Boo focused and trotted toward them with his usual flapping ears and open, happy mouth. When he reached his kids, he stood calmly and relaxed, no longer fidgeting, for as long as the children petted him. It was as if they were all healing one another.

Between his visits, I thought I'd try putting Boo to work in my dog-training consultations. An unflappable dog can be very helpful in work with dogs who have developed dog–dog reactivity. In the face of a reactive dog—even one subthreshold, who is not overtly reacting— Boo adopts several typical, calming social facilitation signals, like casual sniffing, turning away when things get too difficult for him and moving very slowly past the subject dog, as if he's walking through pudding. This allows the handler of the reactive dog to work with the dog in safe proximity to a dog like Boo who does all the right things. If I kept the subject dog subthreshold and brought Boo into the mix at a good distance, performing his best calming signals (as if he'd read Turid Rugaas's book), my clients were able to learn how to help their dogs through what would normally be a reactive moment. This work was invaluable and sometimes funny.

I remember when Boo came with me to meet a client on the West Point compound one Saturday. This was post-9/11, and there were additional security checkpoints in place. Because we'd just come from the AATEA class, all the paraphernalia were in the car, including a giant blow-up Bozo the Clown, battery-operated animals like the oinking pig, and Pipi-Max, the peeing and barking dog. Pipi-Max started his automated barking when I hit a speed bump at the entrance to the compound; and as the very stern-looking military fellow leaned into the open hatch for inspection, he was greeted with the maniacal, barking Pipi-Max and a mysteriously moving Bozo, as Boo came out from behind the clown to poke his nose at the officer from the middle of this chaos. The amused officer smiled at Boo and said, "Aren't you cute." Boo seemed to be able to make anyone smile.

Boo loved what he was doing, especially his Blythedale visits, where often it was because of his limitations that he was able to help the kids. On one visit, a girl came into the common area using a prone stander. Children who can't stand on their own risk underdevelopment of hips, knees and related muscle groups if they spend all their time seated or lying down. Prone standers allow these kids to stand upright without having to support themselves. The standers are usually on wheels, so kids can move around, and have large bases, but an apparatus like that can be particularly terrifying to dogs. Imagine yourself as a dog, then picture a looming construct of metal, plastic and wood containing a silent, immobile child gliding toward you. You might find it a little scary, but not Boo, who couldn't see the looming construct particularly well and so didn't get particularly worried. He heard it and seemed to worry for a moment about his toes until it stopped in front of him.

Boo and the girl started playing with a squeaking, rubber sneaker. She would toss the toy, he would dash to it as if it were the most exciting thing in the world and then he'd sniff it and walk away. His disappointment when he realized it was just a sneaker, or perhaps astonishment that anybody expected him to do anything with it—after all, she'd thrown it, so she should come pick it up, right?—kept the girl laughing the entire time, as he sauntered off aimlessly in another direction while I ran to pick up the sneaker so they could repeat the whole exercise again.

After everyone tired of the sneaker toss, Boo and I made our way around the room and found a teenage boy carrying a laptop and looking interested in all the dogs. As I stopped Boo to ask the boy whether he wanted to pet the dog, the teenager opened his computer and typed something briefly before the laptop spoke for him and said yes.

I felt my heart twist in my chest as I remembered Chuck typing on his computer to speak just like this. Boo and I sat down right away. The boy clearly enjoyed petting Boo's thick, super-soft fur, but he didn't say anything. Once I thought I heard a bit of a laugh, but I suspect it was just Boo's snorting as he snuzzled the boy in return for the kind petting. One of the caregivers came over and encouraged the boy to speak to Boo without the help of his computer, but he seemed reluctant, preferring to keep petting Boo silently. I pulled out the big guns and put Boo on my lap in bug-a-Boo position for maximum clowning effect, hoping it would get the boy talking. Although he didn't speak, he laughed out loud as he continued to pet Boo and fiddle with the little feet jutting out in all directions. Of course, Boo sat there with his usual silly grin, eating up all the attention.

Although Boo is pretty comfortable in that position, he can only hold it for so long, so when he began to squirm after a few minutes, I placed him back on the floor. The boy gave one last pet to Boo, and a look of intense effort covered his face before he said out loud, with a look of personal triumph, "Boo."

In that moment, I felt in a strange way that Boo was fulfilling, if belatedly, my desire to train him to work with my brother. A wave of gratitude washed over me, and I realized that by being less than anybody thought he should be, Boo had once again become more than anybody thought he ever could be.

11
Challenges and Changes

As Boo's confidence soared, so did his successes in a variety of settings. In addition to his regular visits, he was starting to take over a few of Dante's visits. At over eleven years old, the big dog was slowing down, and letting Boo step in for a few of his visits gave Dante the ability to move gracefully into semiretirement. Although the BOCES visits were one of Dante's first visits, and the one where he worked his magic with the little boy who was deaf and blind, he was no longer able to deal as easily with the long drive. Zany time would always be his favorite, but now Boo began taking over a few of these visits for his big brother.

Boo's greatest talent is snuzzling, and this, plus the fact that he loved to come in close for petting, made him perfect for the BOCES visits. Some of the kids were too disabled to watch any of his silly lap-sitting behaviors or his version of fetch, which I think is called "You threw it, I found it, you go get it," but what helped them most was simply having a furry dog to pet and snuggle with—or, in Boo's case, snuzzle.

The biggest troubles Boo had on these visits

were with the kids who didn't respond at all. He didn't seem to understand unresponsiveness. This is hard for many dogs, and keeping them close to an unresponsive client requires a great deal of creativity on the part of the handler. When a dog is not responded to, he tends to walk away. It is one of the greatest forms of negative punishment we have. Just look away from the barking dog, and he will often stop and look for something better to do, but that can backfire on a visit with expressionless clients. I could manage to get Boo to move into kids and give them the old ear snuzzle and maybe a bit of a face sniff, but if he got no reaction from the kids, my only recourse was to lure him to stay in place.

However, when a dog refuses to visit a person or remain by that person, it's always good to ask whether the dog is trying to tell us something. Usually, the answer is yes. In early years of visiting, Dante taught me that when a dog shows a lack of interest in visiting someone, there is probably a very good reason. One time, Dante and I were visiting in the recreation room of a senior center. The seniors were in a large circle around the room, and Dante and I, along with another team, were visiting each person one by one. At one point, Dante chose to blow past one woman in the circle, moving quickly on to the next smiling resident. I figured the other team would visit her as they came around, and if

Dante had a reason, I certainly wasn't going to force him to visit someone.

After the visit, I was about to apologize to the team leader for missing that woman when she beat me to it and asked, "How did you know that one resident didn't want to be visited? I was about to tell you when you guys just went past her!" As it turned out, the woman was not interested in visiting the dogs and was only there to accompany her friend.

All I could do was shrug, point to Dante, and say, "I had no idea, but apparently Dante got the memo."

The few other times when Dante refused to visit clients were also prompted by good reasons. In the middle of a rousing game of fetch with a boy in a wheelchair wearing a sturdy helmet, Dante went to retrieve the ball and stopped dead in his tracks on his way back. Dropping the ball about three feet from the boy, Dante froze and refused to approach the child. Within seconds, the boy was in full seizure, the helmet keeping his neck stable and preventing him from banging his head against the high back of his wheelchair. Over his visiting career, Dante predicted two other seizures in addition to this one, each time stopping midvisit and refusing to interact with the child until the seizure passed. Although scientists aren't sure how dogs detect the approach of a seizure, they suspect that cues may include changes in the person's muscle tension, facial expression, breathing or scent. In the cases of the seizure episodes and the woman who wanted nothing to do with the dogs, I had to bow to Dante's abilities to see social cues and expressions more quickly and clearly than I could.

As a result of this understanding, when Boo would tell me in his own way on a BOCES visit that he was done visiting with a client who was unresponsive, I didn't try to force the visit. Instead, I sought to set up visits that made the best of the child's ability to work with Boo by creatively incorporating the various structures in the room to allow for the maximum level of interactions. Because many of the kids were in wheelchairs, and Boo comes in at just under two feet at the shoulders, we had to find a way to elevate him. Dante, a much taller dog with greater agility, could simply go up on his hind legs, place his paws on a chair next to the wheelchair and be at the perfect height for visiting, but when Boo tried that position, he'd usually topple over. On the few occasions when he held that position for brief durations, he was still too short. Luckily, there were piles of tumbling mats stacked around the room, and if the caregiver positioned the child's wheelchair next to a stack of mats, Boo could simply walk on the mats straight toward the child at perfect arm, head or ear height. The children who could reach out did so easily with him in this position, and the ones who were less responsive could still receive the trademark Boo snuzzle, especially in the ear—Boo's favorite. Because he was comfortable up on the mats, when a child was unresponsive, Boo was able to linger a little longer in case he might rouse some reactions, which he sometimes did.

Time after time, Boo rivaled much smarter dogs on visits with his calm, gentle presence. There were no real tricks Boo could do to entertain—no fetching for fun, no wave, no crawl, no patty-cake, no bow—nothing, really, except disarm just about anyone with his easygoing, inviting little look. Boo, together with his younger brother, Porthos, taught me that in fact, sometimes being smart gets in a visiting dog's way.

Porthos was one of the fastest learners I have ever taught. A puzzle-working genius, he, like his predecessor Atticus, quickly learned which cues he needed to comply with and which ones he could ignore. But just as Boo showed me that the dullest dog sometimes makes the best visiting dog, Porthos showed me the other side of the truth: the smartest dog doesn't necessarily make the best visiting dog. Knowing what I had in store for Porthos, I started taking him out almost right away for socialization and fun. He went on adventures with me at least three or four times a week to strip malls, vet's offices, parks and other places to meet people, and he did well with everybody: kids, adults, seniors, other dogs, you name it. At about five months, he began getting carsick, but with a little Dramamine, that problem went away. At ten months, though, in contrast to Boo, who never had any reactivity issues, Porthos began reacting badly to other dogs. Dog–dog reactivity always reminds me of classic cowboy duels. First comes the standoff, then the decision to react or not react, and finally the shooting, the rumble or the retreat. I remember clearly when it hit me that we had a problem brewing. Porthos was attending class with me, and a male rottweiler just about Porthos's size, age and temperament entered the classroom.

I saw eighty-five-pound Porthos eye the rottie and bark. "Woof, woof," he said in a baritone voice, which I think meant, "Yo mamma."

The rottie responded, "Woof, woof, woof." Probably about ten pounds bigger but with the same baritone range, I think he was saying, "You and what army?"

They simultaneously hurtled toward each other. It was all quickly redirected, controlled and contained, and both boys made it through the rest of the class politely, but I suspect that by the end of the hour, the rottie's handler was just as exhausted as I was.

Dog reactivity would be a serious impediment to visiting, so we began working to counter it before it developed into a huge problem. Using a combination of healthy doses of desensitizing and operant conditioning, I gave Porthos lovely treats every time he saw another dog at a distance that didn't make him nuts (or in technical terms, he stayed subthreshold). I rewarded him for any of the following behaviors: no reaction (remaining controlled and mostly calm), looking at the dog and then checking in with me or performing any canine social facilitation signal (looking away, sniffing the ground, yawning, sitting and so on). We got to the point where if he was surprised by the appearance of another dog who might dare to look directly at him, Porthos would offer a giant-sized woof, remember that there might be something else he was supposed to do instead and look up at me for further direction. It wasn't perfect but it was progress.

As Porthos came more under my control, unfortunately, my health was doing the opposite. My joints were starting to give me greater and greater trouble again, and this time my hips were, too. I had no joints left to open doors, and bending to pick up things was often painful. I started to think Porthos could have a dual career:

mobility assist dog on my bad days and therapeutic visiting dog on my good days. With his strength and size (almost twenty-eight inches at the withers, where the back, neck and shoulders meet), his intelligence and his focus, he had all the right makings for a mobility assist dog on those days when my body was just not cooperating.

Porthos made super-fast progress on the work Boo just couldn't get through when I was training him for Chuck. Picking up and bringing me things was a breeze for Porthos—so much so that when he was the demo dog during a few workshops I led, he would spend the day surreptitiously removing various participants' pocketbooks, wallets or cell phones from the owners' purses or jackets and bringing them back to me. I kept having to interrupt the workshop, hold up a wallet or cell phone and ask the amazed crowd who owned it. If I'd been a magician, Porthos would have been a brilliant assistant, and if I'd had nefarious intentions, Porthos would have made a great pickpocket partner.

Porthos also had an extraordinary ability to make logical connections. I taught him a game in which he would go find his toy on command. On one skunk-chasing adventure, Dante took off, and when he didn't return in his usual ten minutes, I started worrying. Searching as far as I could with no results, I was grasping at straws when I told Porthos, "Find Dante." It was almost a joke because I'd never asked Porthos to find either of the other dogs, just his puzzle toy, and never outside, so when he took off in the opposite direction, I simply assumed he hadn't understood. Still, I had no choice but to follow him. I was about to take him back to the house when, sure enough, there was Dante bounding toward us. I never would have thought to search in that location. Porthos earned his kibble that day. Dante earned a skunk wash.

Porthos picked up other skills that he would need as a mobility assist dog incredibly quickly, too. His happy tug could hoist me up from the floor if I fell or was sitting on the floor and having trouble getting up. I thought back to the days in New York when I had fallen several times on the subway. If I needed to take the subway again, Porthos would be able to help me up. His size also made him the perfect carry dog: he could wear a backpack that contained the contents of my purse so I could escape the pain I usually got from carrying one.

Despite some behavioral road bumps, I was well on the way to achieving with Porthos what I had failed to accomplish with Boo: training a mobility assist dog. Porthos's public access work was going well: his out-and-about skills with people were great, and by now he was even good with strange dogs. The next step was to help him conquer his greatest fear: claustrophobia. Porthos's biggest anxiety, even worse than his former dog reactivity, arose when I asked him to go under a table, in an elevator, between me and the grocery store shelves to make room for other shoppers—anywhere he had very little room to maneuver.

But even there, we made enough progress in getting him happier with smaller spaces that I felt it was time for us to revisit my old colleagues who were specialists in service dog training for more specific directions on training the skills of a service dog. On that trip, Porthos screamed for his life like I had never heard another dog scream before or since and never wish to hear again. Porthos didn't want to go under the trainer's grooming table, but instead of slowly luring him or potentially shaping him to a position under the table, the trainer said, "Look, you have to show him who's boss."

My face was probably expressionless like melting gelatin as I tried to process what was happening in that instant to my screaming dog. I had no time to say anything before she said, "He'll get over it," then dragged him and pushed him under the table, getting the leash caught around his leg while he fought and screamed.

"I, uh, he doesn't—maybe if . . . if I just lure

him. . . ." I tried. I was horrified by what she was doing to my dog, but I was the subordinate here, the upstart, and she was the trainer with twenty years of experience. I didn't know how or where to find the strength to stop her. Although it was clear that Porthos was in pain, I feared the trainer would accuse me of anthropomorphizing—for some old-school dog trainers, there's no greater insult than to hurl that remark at a trainer who considers an animal's emotions along with their actions. It means, in their minds, *You're treating this animal as if it were human.*

"He has to know you mean it," she snapped, still wrestling. When she finally finished, Porthos was sitting under the grooming table, body rigid, eyes wide and unblinking, face pulled together as tightly as was physically possible, lips pursed, ears flat back against his head and tail tucked so far under himself that he was sitting on it, the tip looking like it was trying to make a shield for his gut. "See?" she said. "He's just fine."

He was not fine. That night, he refused to go under the kitchen table for dinner. When we returned to agility class, he wanted nothing to do with the tunnel. Then, I came home to find that he had plucked all the fur off his tail. Yes, that experience with force so terrified him that he began mutilating himself. When I took him to the vet to check out the tail, we also found an eight-inch abrasion under his leg where the leash had caught when he was screaming.

I only wish that I had not allowed my fears of being ridiculed to hold me silent as my dog was being harmed.

That experience scarred poor Porthos, but it also changed me and the way I'd come to think about anthropomorphizing and training. The notion that other animals don't have the emotional capacity of humans is an arrogant idea. Modern medical testing has shown us via pet scans, fMRIs, the measurement of neuro-transmitters and hormones that the emotional portion of our human brains (also known as the mammalian or limbic brain, which evolved much earlier than our frontal lobe) is almost identical to those of other mammals. As I sat and looked at Porthos's hairless tail and felt the abrasion under his leg, I knew that from that moment on, I would dance naked (not literally) around the bonfires of anthropomorphizing. I am a human, and this is how I understand the world around me, *and* because my dogs feel the emotions I do, I will use my experience to attempt to understand the emotional state of the animal. I will gladly stand face to face with any person who claims this is just anthropomorphizing and remind them that when they talk about dogs being dominant or submissive or adhere to the idea that the act of being on the bed is a measurement of power, *they* are the ones making giant, anthropomorphic leaps with no basis in fact. In order to teach Boo, I had to understand what he felt, and to help Porthos, I ought to have been willing to stand up and say, "That dog is in pain and afraid."

In the wake of his response to this trauma, I shelved Porthos's service career and worked only on getting him ready for a career as a visiting dog. Porthos passed his evaluation, and now all three of my dogs were registered Pet Partners.

I chose to start Porthos's visits slowly, with BOCES, because theirs had become fairly controlled and contained, and the last few visits with Boo had been consistently well organized. We would typically have two teams, visiting only one child at a time out in the large recreation area, where I knew Porthos would be more comfortable and have room to work away from the other dog.

I had forgotten that these visits occasionally reverted to the loud, boisterous, zany madhouse of sound and movement that dominated in the early days when Dante and I first began visiting there, depending on the staff working that day. Things started going downhill right from the start. Just out of the car, Porthos saw Olympia, Dante's girlfriend. With his big, deep-chested bark, Porthos got everyone's attention. After many pass-bys, when Cindy and I just walked our dogs past each other until they were bored, we were ready to go into the facility. Of course, our usual point person wasn't there, and before I could get my backpack off, Porthos and I were descended upon by three children, all accompanied by their caregivers. Handsome Porthos, with the look of a golden retriever but all black, could be a magnet. But as the six people surrounded him, he began throwing look aways as quickly as he could: he kept anxiously turning his head away from unwanted attention in an attempt to tell the descending crowd, in dogspeak, that he needed room. Realizing they didn't speak dog, I translated, "Please approach one at a time. We need to visit only one child at a time."

My pleas were ignored by the six humans huddled around the now-frantic dog. One of the caregivers reached out and pushed Porthos's face back toward the children in an attempt to force him to interact face-to-face with the child. I had an instant panic, expecting the inevitable.

Luckily I was able to intervene, and tragedy was avoided. I said, "Until we can do this one child at a time, he will not visit anyone." I escorted Porthos across the room, and he and I spent the rest of our time at that visit just working around the room on simple commands and focus games. Cindy and Olympia picked up the extra slack and completed the visit on their own.

Clearly, I had to be more careful about the visits I chose for Porthos. He was not Boo with his go-anywhere attitude, and Porthos was not the fly-through-the-air Dante. With Dante's full retirement looming on the horizon, I hoped that Porthos could step in and help Boo pick up the slack. Porthos tried a visit to Danielle's third-grade classroom, but although he loved the kids, he wasn't thrilled by the sounds of the classroom, barking at the loudspeaker and the grinding noises the heating unit made. It was also clear to me that although he was under control around other dogs, he still wasn't completely comfortable with some of them. Visits with multiple dogs set him up for elevated stress, so I needed to find solo visits for him, but all of H.A.R.T.'s visits were multiple-dog visits, which ruled them out for him. While I tried to come up with a solution for Porthos, I continued to move Boo the trooper into more of Dante's visits.

My spring visiting semester ended with a bundle of mixed emotions. I felt great pride in Dante's years of visiting and in Boo's incredible metamorphosis from the confused, clumsy dog that nobody believed in to the gifted visiting dog with butterfly wings. I also felt regretful that I may have pushed Porthos too far too fast into something he might not even want simply because he was smart and cooperative.

All of this, however, took a backseat when Dad was diagnosed with cancer. He was seventy-nine and had smoked heavily almost three quarters of his life and drank just as heavily. He was unlikely to have come down with a little bit o' cancer. The disease would probably take him quickly and hard.

Mom, Dad and I were finally in a good place in our relationship. We could kid around with one another, and we had common interests, solid boundaries and a forgiveness that was no less real for being unspoken. At the end of May, four years after Chuck's death, I flew to Florida to visit my father, suspecting he wouldn't last the year. When I got there and started going along with them to chemo and radiation every other day, it finally sank in how bad this was.

Dad's energy was pretty low, and on one quiet, treatment-free afternoon, he sat out on the lanai watching me do a few walking laps in the pool (I still couldn't comfortably put my head under water). The alligator prowling on the other side of the fence made me a bit nervous, so I got out of the pool, and Dad and I just sat together, looking out over the pond. We chatted about the golf course, the alligators who lived there and other trivial things until he hesitated a bit and said something about not living as good a life as he could have.

I said, "I know. We all have regrets."

Unable to make eye contact, he said, "I have some pretty big ones. I did things to you that I don't know can be forgiven."

My limbs began to shake, and I felt that old tightness in my chest. Fighting back tears, I said, "None of us are perfect. Anyone who tells you they have no regrets isn't being honest. Life isn't and shouldn't be about being perfect."

Dad was staring straight ahead, his eyes seemingly fixed on the alligator. There was a long silence. Knowing that I needed to say more, I continued, "It's about what we do to fix the mistakes we've made that matters."

Like so many dogs I worked with who are worried or afraid, Dad's body was stiff, and he kept his eyes fixed straight ahead. Still unable to look at me, he seemed to be holding his breath to hold the rest of himself still. Then, when he had enough control, he said, "I've tried to make things better."

"I know. You've done a lot to fix things."

He had been sober for over twenty years and done as much as he could to redeem himself for my mother and for me. He had completely altered how he interacted with me, keeping a physical distance, softening his impatience and judgment while attempting some encouragement.

He had remained faithful to Mom and doted on her. In short, he had gone from an impatient, belligerent, sarcastically insulting tyrant to a patient, encouraging, thoughtful man.

I could see years of guilt and regret ease out of him as he finally exhaled, slowly letting his whole body release from the rigid control he used to contain his emotions. Then, he said, "I'm glad."

Both of us remained silent and still for a little bit, struggling to contain ourselves and fighting hard not to cry. There was not going to be a magic wand that made the past disappear, but there was repentance and forgiveness, and this was the closest anyone in my family ever came to saying, "I'm sorry" or "I forgive you." I suspect it was the closest he ever came to absolution.

I had spent enough time in Al-Anon and with recovering alcoholics to know that what he did all those years ago was a symptom of his disease, not a function of his character. I had spent enough time working with reactive and aggressive dogs to know just how much all our actions are driven by chemicals in the brain, chemicals we're only now beginning to understand. My time with Boo had given me the patience and wisdom to accept imperfection in dogs, but now I realized that it had given me the patience and wisdom to accept imperfection in humans, too. This gift from Boo was the final piece in my recovery, the piece that allowed me to forgive the man who so deeply wounded me and offer him the unconditional love I had learned from Atticus.

At the end of that visit, I knew I would never see my father again. I also knew that when he died, I could truly mourn him. In an odd twist of fate that mirrored his father's passing, Dad went into the hospital the day after my birthday that year. He died a week later.

A month after Dad's funeral, Porthos had a bad night that kept us both up until four o'clock in the morning. He seemed to want to vomit but couldn't. His compulsive response to his discomfort was to eat everything that was not nailed down—the same obsessive-compulsive disorder pica (the compulsion to eat things that aren't food) that he had shown over the training anxiety. I followed him around the house all night, walked him around the yard when he indicated he had to go out in the hope that it would relieve his discomfort, and tried to comfort him with TTouch circles and lifts. TTouch, a system of training, healing and communication designed by Linda Tellington-Jones to help humans have a deeper and more compassionate relationship with their animals through massage-like touch, has been around for about as long as I have. I was hoping that the circles and lifts I was doing would help Porthos's body take care of itself until I could get him to his regular vet.

When we did get to the vet's the next morning, the Wednesday before Thanksgiving, they all looked at me and said, "You look awful." I looked like hell, and of course Porthos (pumped up by his own adrenaline from seeing his buddies) frolicked around the office, showing no sign of any distress, stealing purses and boots that belonged to the staff. I was instructed to fast him for the rest of the day and give him bland boiled chicken and rice for dinner so his gut could rest. By ten o'clock that night, he was repeating the pacing, panting and frantic eating from the night before. Again, we were up until dawn on Thanksgiving morning before he could vomit again. This behavior repeated itself on Friday night, and by Saturday, he was visibly sick. No amount of excitement at seeing his friends was going to perk him up at the vet's as it had on Wednesday. He was admitted, X-rays were taken and an obstruction was found.

Later that afternoon, he underwent emergency surgery to remove a bezoar the size of a full toupee. Since Porthos was apparently at the tipping point of bloat each night, Cindy pexied his stomach to the abdominal wall during the operation. This procedure attaches the stomach to the wall of the abdomen so the stomach can't twist during bloat and cause torsion. I spent the rest of the weekend worrying and crying. I had lost Chuck in '02, Atticus in '03, Merlin the cat in '04, Tara the cat in '05, Dad in '06—I was supposed to have one loss a year not two!

Luckily, Porthos came home early the next week. He had a slow recovery and eventually developed a scar almost identical to Lawrence's.

The rest of that year, I chose to coast through Boo's and Dante's visits, keeping them fairly easy, not committing to too many a month, not adding anything new. It was spring of the next year when Porthos seemed ready to get back into the game. Remembering his trouble during previous visits, I wasn't sure where to place him until one of my students brought an opportunity to my attention. She'd started taking her dog to visit at the Maryknoll Sisters Nursing Home, a retirement home for Maryknoll nuns, but then realized her dog wasn't meant to be a visiting dog, and Maryknoll was looking for a replacement.

I remembered back to when I first started visiting with Dante. At first, I'd wanted to take him to visit the elderly to pay homage to my grandmother. Gramma J had been such a strong support for me, the only support besides my brother. For years after she moved in with us, she tried to make my life a little easier. She came to live with us just before I fell out of a tree and broke my leg. It was a full break of the left femur, and back then the standard treatment was six to eight weeks of traction to maintain the growth of the broken leg so it didn't turn out shorter than the other one. Traction for more than a month was a prison sentence for a four-year-old. While I was in the hospital, my family was moving into a new house, so my parents couldn't visit often, and hospitals didn't allow children to visit, so my siblings weren't allowed to come visit at all. But Gramma J came every day, bringing me a stuffed animal each time; real animals weren't on the visitors' list in those days, so it was the best she could do.

After I got back from the hospital, Gramma J continued working with me to teach me how to walk again. She didn't scold me for not using the crutches because they scared the crap out of me. Instead, she devised another plan for me: to walk around her tall bed, holding onto the sides for stability. Much like my work with Boo forced me to think outside the box, so did she.

Because I hadn't been able to thank her before she died, I felt that giving back to seniors with Dante would be a way I could thank her posthumously. As much as I loved that idea, however, it was not for Dante. At his size and with his ebullience, he was sometimes too much for them. He could easily tear the skin of a frail elderly client by giving paw too roughly or knock someone down if he turned too quickly to say hello. But Maryknoll had all the right elements for Porthos: it would be quiet, without too much activity, and he loved older women.

This was my first visit out on my own, without the support of the retitled H.E.A.R.T. (Human–Animal Educational and Relational Therapy) Programs. Diane Pennington moved away to be closer to family, and perhaps it was time for me to have some distance, too. Porthos and I were to visit the fourth floor at Maryknoll, reserved for the sisters with medical or cognitive issues who required more assistance than those in the independent living areas on the lower floors. Naturally, when we got to the lobby to start our first visit, we came upon . . . the elevator. Porthos had never recovered from his traumatic experience at the trainer's and was still afraid of going into small, dark spaces. He sat down seven feet from the torture device and looked away slowly and deliberately. No matter what I used to lure him into the big box of doom, he wasn't having it. The flooding of forcing him under the grooming table had only strengthened his fear of small, dark spaces, and he was so smart that he easily made the connection between anywhere enclosed, dark and small.

I tried standing in the elevator with Linda, my

recreational specialist for these visits, both of us cooing happily to Porthos for several minutes, but he refused to even look in our direction. Eventually, Linda suggested that we take the stairs. It was a long, hard climb for me and my aching joints, but it was the only way Porthos was going to get to the fourth floor, so up we went. (I couldn't send him up with somebody else while I took the elevator because I have to go where he goes on a visit. The leash should never leave my hand.) Once we finally made it to the fourth floor, Porthos had a lovely time saying hello to the sisters and snuffling his nose up their sweater sleeves in search of delicious tissues. He was happy to go for walks with them up and down the well-lit hallway or be brushed, in the case of the sisters with better motor skills, by the ZoomGroom, an ergonomically designed rubber brush that was easy for the sisters to hold and easy on Porthos, who was always happy to be brushed. When he saw the ZoomGroom and knew he was going to get brushed, he would stand with his giant mouth gaping and tongue hanging to one side as if he was saying, "A little to the left, please. Thaaat's the spot," while he pumped up and down with his back legs in gracious approval.

Although the sisters adored him—Sister Ann Elise even sang songs to him—each new trip to Maryknoll revealed new things that unnerved

Porthos. One of our visits took us down a secondary hallway, where we encountered some lighting fixtures that left puddles of light on the shiny, multicolored tiles. He balked as if I were asking him to walk through a minefield. With a limited color range, much less visual acuity than humans and a surface behind the retina that reflects light around the inside of their eyes to allow for better night vision (this is called the tapetum lucidum), dogs just don't see the world the same way we do. So, it didn't surprise me that a strange lighting system could be a trigger. Very high-contrast lighting on an already perplexingly patterned floor could easily look to a dog like a strange Escher painting with various layers that just don't seem to make sense, leaving him confused and potentially afraid.

Although Porthos loved the nuns, he found the environment at Maryknoll a constant source of anxiety. I began to wonder whether this was the right job for him. The answer came easily from, of course, Porthos, as we were leaving for our last visit of the spring semester. He knew, as all the dogs did, exactly what was going to happen when I picked up his visiting backpack. At the sight of the backpack, Dante and Boo would dance around with happy noises and happy howling, respectively, but when Porthos saw the bag this time, he walked alongside me like a condemned man. As I locked the door before we headed to the car, Porthos lay down on the deck and exposed his belly as if to say, "Please, Mom, I don't wanna." The sisters were counting on us, and it was simply too late to cancel. I encouraged him into the car and promised it would be a short visit. We stayed a half hour instead of our usual hour, and I let Linda know that Boo would be coming next time.

I had to face Porthos's medical issues head-on. His near-bloat episodes began to increase during the summer months, and I was injecting him more frequently with metoclopramide to help his stomach churn and pass whatever he had eaten, good or bad. It kept him out of the hospital, but he wasn't thriving and always looked like he was in a yucky mood. His brothers were the light of his life, yet he had started behaving snarkily toward them, barking at them, snarling at them, not wanting anything to do with them. Finally, we did an endoscopy and found signs of inflammatory bowel disease. He was officially and forever retired from all work and put on new medications that controlled his bowel inflammation and kept his anxiety levels in check. It was much less important to me that he be a visiting dog than a happy dog.

Boo was not only taking over for many of Dante's visits, but also he would now, as I promised Linda, take over Porthos's, too. Where Porthos was the bouncy, in-your-face, let-me-eat-your-tissue dog, Boo was the quiet, hey-how-ya-doin' dog, and it was interesting to see the different kinds of reactions the two got from the sisters.

Sister Jean, for example, was ninety-four when Porthos and I started visiting. She was deep in the clutches of Alzheimer's and not particularly interested in the big, bouncy dog. She came to the visits clutching a stuffed animal, staring at nothing and never speaking. Linda indicated that there was very little anyone could do to get through to her to extract a positive reaction. Porthos was certainly never able to elicit a response from her.

Boo was up for the challenge, though. I asked Linda for a wheeled desk chair without arms. I sat down in the chair, scooped Boo up in an incredibly immodest way (for both me and him), plopped him on my lap, almost fell out of the chair (which would have been a very different kind of entertainment for the sisters) and scooted over to Sister Jean, parking as close as I could without wheeling over any feet. Scooching Boo over in her direction, I gently laid his head on her lap where, nestled in comfort, feet sticking out in every direction, he grinned the goofiest grin imaginable. I supported him so most of his weight remained on me while Linda helped Sister Jean stroke his soft little ears and nestle her fingers into his thick neck fur.

There was an undeniable glimmer in her eyes as she touched Boo, whether from the petting, Linda's touch or the odd feeling of having a warm animal suddenly on her lap. There was no way to know exactly what did what, but with each visit, Sister Jean became more responsive to Boo. She stopped bringing her stuffed animals, she started to reach out for Boo on her own and at last she began saying, "Boo! Boo!" occasionally during her visits. It was the first time in years that anyone had heard her speak out loud.

According to a 2004 study presented at the International Conference on Human–Animal Interactions, AAT for Alzheimer's patients has been shown to improve speech and attention span significantly and to decrease drastic changes in mental state. A growing body of research, including studies by the American Public Health Association, also reported that in medical settings, such as nursing homes, pet visits reduce patients' stress and enhance their psychological well-being.

On one visit, Linda said, "When Boo puts his head in Sister Jean's lap or nuzzles her hand, she gets the most beautiful smile, a smile she never gets otherwise. It's wonderful to see her so happy. When we ask if she's enjoying the visit, she'll nod and let us help her move her arm so she can hug Boo." The heartrending irony is that it was just a few years earlier that as the director of recreation for the Maryknoll Sisters' retirement center, Sister Jean founded the facility's AAT program, breaking new ground by bringing cats, bunnies and birds into the facility to comfort and inspire the other sisters. It was only fitting that she would later be helped by her own innovation as we took her work to the next level by bringing in dogs.

Jean wasn't the only sister on whom Boo had a great effect. There was also Eleanor. Even though she was often unable to get out of bed, she would rush on visiting days to join the two dozen sisters awaiting Boo's arrival in the larger recreation room. She would take him for a walk halfway down the hallway and then ask to go back to sit down, tired from the much-needed exercise. Then, she stayed for the rest of the visit to watch Boo practice his skills for his next renewal test or looking at his photo album that I had filled with pictures of him with Dante, Atticus, the cats and whatever else I thought would be fun to add.

Sister Ann Elise continued singing about the visiting dog, and now that she'd had some practice, it was even easier for her to weave Boo's name into the songs. "How Much Is That Doggie in the Window?" for example, became "How Much Is That Boo-Boo in the Window?" On one visit, when she was beginning to decline in health, she grabbed onto Boo's leash when I said we had to go visit other sisters. She didn't want to let him go, and she actually gave me a good couple hard slugs to the leg when I said he had to come with me. Linda rescued me and explained to Sister Ann Elise that Boo would be back to see her again, but somehow Sister Ann Elise just didn't want the visit to end. She passed away before our next visit, and I wonder if she might have known all along that this was going to be the last time she saw Boo.

Even Sister Dorothy, who had a lifelong fear of dogs, was eventually disarmed enough by Boo's sweet, charming nature that she was willing to pet him, take him for a walk and give him treats. On these walks up and down the hallway, Sister Dorothy would regale Boo with stories of the neighborhood dogs who scared her as a child. "It was a big, brown, scary dog," she would tell Boo, "not like you." She still had a small fear of dogs, though, and when she would try to give Boo a treat, she would squeal with a mix of fear and delight as soon as his nose reached her open palm and she would drop the treat to the floor before his mouth could touch her hand. Confused, Boo would sniff the air, wondering what happened to the treat, and then follow the scent to the floor and happily gobble it up, at which point Sister Dorothy would continue her stories.

• • •

Boo's work with the sisters was bringing us small miracles with each visit, but there was a bigger miracle happening at home. When we first got married, Lawrence had made it clear that the issue of children was permanently off the table, to the point that I had only ever broached the subject once or twice more in the eleven years we'd been together. That old hesitation to ask for what I wanted still nibbled away at me like a patch of rust that just wouldn't go away. I was like Sister Dorothy and Boo's treats: whenever I came close to asking for something, I would pull back in terror.

But one day, out of the blue, Lawrence started talking about the kids of a friend from high school, and I just broke down in tears. I realized that all this time, although I'd kept myself from thinking about it, I had hoped we would have a child of our own. And now I had to accept that that simply wasn't a possibility. Then, through my tears, I heard Lawrence say something I just couldn't believe: "We should have a baby."

I was shocked. "But what about your fears of becoming your father?" I asked. "The things you've always been worried about?"

"I know I am not my biological father," he said. In eleven years of marriage, he'd never beaten me or the dogs. He didn't have a hair-trigger temper like his biological father and

301

wasn't a violent person. "I won't be like him, and you would be a great mother."

As much as this change of heart took me by surprise, I knew Lawrence well enough to know that when it comes to making decisions, he is like a tectonic plate that seems to move suddenly but has been contemplating its next move for years. He mulls things over quietly to himself, assessing and reassigning his life until he reaches a conclusion. Only then does he share it. Although it was still difficult for me to believe that I could be great at anything (save, perhaps, dog training), I knew that my recovery and the peace I had made with Dad would make me a much better mother than I would have ever been before.

When I thought about the family we'd created and cared for over the years—Atticus, Dante, Boo, Porthos, Tara and Merlin—I had every faith that Lawrence and I could do this. Together, we'd already proven ourselves to be wonderful parents to our canine and feline kids. It was finally the right time to start a family of our own, and we agreed that we would move heaven and earth to have a child.

Within a month, Lawrence found a fertility specialist in Connecticut. Filled with hope, we made an appointment, knowing that with our various medical issues and eleven years of not getting pregnant with no active contraception in place, we would probably need some help. During the days before the appointment, we talked excitedly, if cautiously, about the possibilities that were ahead of us. But although the clinic was warm and inviting, the doctor was not. He didn't put his BlackBerry down once during our interview.

"So, you're how old?" he asked after we sat down and introduced ourselves. He glanced at the paperwork we filled out, started tapping his foot on the corner of his desk in what felt like annoyance, turned his attention back to his BlackBerry, and said, "It would be unethical for me to help you have a child at your age."

I shut down. I knew plenty of women who had gotten pregnant in their early and mid-forties. Unfortunately, I was so intimidated that I couldn't push for clarification. I wanted to explain that my mid-twenties were dark years for me, that if I had brought a child into the world during that time, I would have done nothing but continue a legacy of dysfunction, but I literally couldn't bring myself to speak.

Lawrence, bless him, tried to come to my rescue. "I should make it clear that we have waited this long because of me. I had good reason to be cautious," he said, "and what we're really hoping to find is just some help in the—"

"Look," said the doctor, returning his gaze to me, "when it comes to reproduction, it's all pretty much on the woman, and timing is critical." His focus went back to his BlackBerry.

All my old conditioning kicked in, and torrents of blame and self-loathing came sweeping over me. The only option this doctor gave us was to find an egg donor, but without insurance coverage for infertility, we didn't have the savings to pay for this treatment. I also feared that if we conceived this way, our child would be doubly cursed by my family: any child of mine was unlikely to be accepted, and a child of mine from a donor was doubly unlikely. I cried the whole way home and then plopped Boo onto my lap for a good snuzzle, letting his thick fur absorb my tears. Porthos came up and presented his fluffy butt to me as if to say, "I know scratching me right there makes everything better." Even Dante did his usual chin-to-forehead lick to remind me that I was not alone.

I started thinking about how no one had really believed in Boo until he proved everyone wrong. I thought about how far Dante had come—the sickly, uncontrolled junkyard dog from Brooklyn who had made good. I realized the dogs were my mirror. I thought, *If Boo could do things no one expected him to do, then why shouldn't I keep trying? The key was for me to concentrate on what could be done rather than being stymied by what couldn't.* I started working with an acupuncturist and contacted my homeopath; they were the only two medical professionals who had helped me through the toughest times of chronic pain, so maybe they had a rabbit up their sleeves for infertility, too. Lawrence and I also started researching other reproductive specialists to get a second opinion. For my own mental health, I turned more of my focus to my business and the visits.

It was time for me to recognize that Dante, who wasn't getting around like he used to, needed a break from the physically demanding SPARC visits. It broke my heart that it was time for him to retire from the visits with which he (and I) started this journey, the visits that made him dance with joy. He loved the various adults with developmental disabilities who attended the SPARC visits, and as the consummate entertainer on those visits, Dante kept them laughing and playing silly games for almost seven years. He spoke on command, balanced on his hind legs like Scooby Doo and chased tennis balls for fetch and fun.

I remember one particularly funny game of chase in a nursery school classroom with low, round tables. Dante went around one of the tables to get the tennis ball, I followed him, he followed me, the leash got caught on the chairs, and round and round we went. I kept trying to unstick the leash, and he kept trying to bring me the ball. I could almost hear comical background music playing as the room full of adults with developmental disabilities hooted and hollered at the goofy dog and his equally goofy human. Even Dante looked like he was laughing at the spectacle we made.

An indisputable vaudevillian, Dante had perfect comic timing and even developed a Three Stooges–esque routine with a clever little sheltie named Cody. One of Cody's many tricks was the ever-popular balance-the-treat-on-the-nose trick. His handler, Liz, would place a cookie on Cody's nose and tell him to stay. After a few seconds, she would tell him to take it, at which point he would flip the cookie into the air, catch it and eat it. Dante and Cody were visiting an adult day-care facility together one afternoon, and while Dante was happily visiting with one client, Liz was setting Cody up to perform his trademark trick several feet away. In a flash, Dante left the side of the man he was visiting and then returned back to him like a rubber band. I heard Liz say, "Heeeeey!" and looked over to see Cody staring cross-eyed at the vacant place on his nose where, moments ago, the cookie had sat waiting for the finale—only to be stolen by Dante. Dante was the picture of innocence as the room erupted in laughter.

When Boo started taking over Dante's SPARC visits, though, I was worried. These visits were a whirlwind, and Boo was not the wild entertainer that Dante was. Boo made people smile and giggle, and although he disarmed many, he was no performer. But as always, Boo proved that just because he wasn't as smart, coordinated or entertaining as Dante, it didn't mean that he couldn't find a way to succeed. The thoughtful, quiet, let-me-sniff-your-ear Boo showed that his big strength on these visits was his love of people. He loved to be up close to the clients. He would also happily trot along with them, walking his adorable circus-pony walk that always made everyone smile, letting the clients feel as though they were walking him. He didn't care if people spoke loudly or had an unusual gait or made unusual gestures with their hands and arms. As Maura said so long ago, "Boo just don't care." When Ena would spasm and scream her scream that meant "I'm so happy to see the dogs," it was an ear-piercing scream from a human perspective, never mind the dog's, and Boo would stand still for a moment, do the doggy equivalent of a shrug, and continue working. Ena's scream has sent many a dog packing from these visits—even Dante had a hard time with these screams and would need some time to recover. But not Boo.

Other activities that were trying for visiting dogs, such as participating in silly party games like the group conga line (a brilliant way to get everyone involved when we had too few dogs for too many clients), didn't bother Boo either. He was practically clueless about the hubbub about him. It was as if he was just out for a walk with his new buddy. Even a pro like Dante would get quite excited by the conga line, and I've seen many other dogs get overwhelmed by the dance and its typical marching, kicking and singing. Not my Boo—he trotted along, ears flopping, just happy to be part of the action.

In the fall of 2007, Boo turned seven years old and was staying the course on his path to becoming the little dog who could.

12

Boo Helps the
Silent Little Boy

When Lawrence and I finally found a local reproductive specialist who said she'd be willing to help, the first step was an FSH (follicle-stimulating hormone) test. During the first half of the menstrual cycle, this hormone, which is critical in women's reproduction, stimulates production of both eggs and the hormone estradiol. As a woman ages, the FSH number goes up and is often used as an indicator that good eggs may not be as plentiful as in younger, more fertile years.

The day I went for my first FSH test to determine where my levels were and whether a baby was even within the realm of possibility also turned out to be the day I met with Penny Weiser to begin setting up our Austin Road Stepping Stones visit. Like twin stars, these parallel paths were locked in each other's orbit. Penny was looking for a visiting dog to work with her special-needs first and second graders for a while, and when she called me, I jumped at the chance.

Lawrence had already taken several tests in preparation for IUI (intrauterine insemination).

Although he had as much sperm as the next guy, his didn't have the best morphology and motility, meaning they weren't all normally formed and weren't always great swimmers. IUI would give the well-developed ones a better chance of finding their appointed target. Meanwhile, I would give myself FSH injections to make sure there were as many targets available as possible. We knew we weren't guaranteed success, but at least we had a plan. The only problem was that when I wasn't on visits, with private clients, at classes or planning for the new children's visit, I was flitting from one mostly icky and sometimes painful test to another.

This was both the absolute worst and best time for me to be taking on a new visit schedule. I was swamped with doctors' appointments, had to pee in a cup every morning, would soon be shooting myself up with FSHs daily and—worst of all by far—had to stop drinking coffee and wine. I would have easily traded two more shots to the belly per day to have my morning coffee.

The rough schedule made this the perfect time to start the Stepping Stones visits. Penny was going to develop educational plans for each student with set goals for Boo's visits. Setting up the games and activities for the kids to match Boo's skills would be an enormous task for me, one that might help take my mind off the fertility quest and let me simply enjoy some time with Boo and the kids.

When we met, Penny described the students' needs. Two of the children had severe ADHD and frequently erupted in tantrums. Another student suffered from genetic diseases that resulted in profoundly disabling complications. One little girl had developmental delays, and one little boy, Marc, had a rare childhood anxiety disorder called selective mutism (until recently called elective mutism).

Selective mutism is characterized by the inability to speak in one or more social settings. Marc, however, didn't speak anywhere, not even at home. He was silent with his mother, his father, his uncle, his uncle's dog, his cousin, his cousin's dog—he was silent everywhere, with everyone. This was very atypical for selective mutism, and because Penny had never taught a student with this problem before, she scoured textbooks and reached out to other educators who could help her find a workable treatment that might help. Although there is a growing pool of information on the disorder, nothing she found worked for Marc. Being a dog lover herself, she wondered whether a therapy dog might coax the little boy to speak, even if just to the dog. With a condition this severe, she knew it was a long shot, but she was willing to try for Marc.

Before I made many elaborate plans for the

group, I wanted to see how they would interact with Boo. It made sense for his first visit to be all about getting them to start communicating with him. The kids had fifth-grade student helpers a couple times a week, and Penny set up Boo's visits to include them so we would have some additional help if we needed it. Boo's visits were also effectively a reward for the fifth graders because they enjoyed him as much as the younger kids did. When we got there, the room was almost full: the seven children in the Stepping Stones program, four fifth-grade helpers, three teacher's aides and Penny.

Boo was his typical, cocktail-party dog working the room in his usual style: feet sniffs, hand licks, a brief ear snuzzle, and in the case of Heather, a petite little girl with a curly head of free-spirited hair who had some developmental delays and seemed perpetually happy, he thought he might gently snack on her barrettes before moving onto the next set of feet. The kids giggled as Boo's gentle, cold nose seemed to wander aimlessly around their heads before he moved on.

The one child who wasn't thrilled was Matthew. Sitting across the room as far from Boo as he could get, Matthew required support from one of the teacher's aides to remain calm. After Boo greeted everybody and all the petting and cooing died down, I plopped Boo on my lap in his usual bug-a-Boo pose, to the delight of the kids. I told his story and showed some of the pictures of Boo with Dante and Atticus so the kids could visualize Boo living at home with brothers, just like many of them did. They were hooked as they watched Boo perched on my lap, his mouth open in a happy, relaxed pant, seeming to look around at nothing and everything all at once. I tried to keep the Boo story short to match the attention spans of the kids, especially the ones with ADHD, but I think I could have gone on for much longer because they were all mesmerized. Even Matthew, still across the room, was now calm, listening, watching everything Boo did.

"Boo is eight, probably older than some of you," I said. "He lives with me, my husband and two other dogs. He likes to snuggle up with me or with his big brother, Dante, on an oversized chair, and he has some special needs, just like you guys." This got their attention. "He doesn't see too well, and he bumps into things a lot. He learns differently from other dogs and moves differently from other dogs, but in the end, he does just fine for himself. His life is full of fun and friends, and he's loved very much."

Once the kids connected with Boo, it was time for the interaction activities. I had made some very simple cards out of standard 8"×10" copy paper, and both sides of each card had a big cue word on it with commands like sit, down, stay, paw and come. I use cards like these on visits to turn simple commands into a game or demonstration. Sometimes I illustrate how dogs follow hand signals by letting a kid show me a card, and then I use the corresponding hand signal to cue the dog. For the Stepping Stones class, I had the children read the cards out loud to Boo while I offered him a nonchalant hand signal or body touch to communicate the command. This can be very empowering for kids because they feel like they've gotten the dog to do something for them all on their own, and it was an intentionally easy game for this first visit.

Penny would hold up one of two cards, either the down or the sit, as each child in turn approached Boo. The student would have to read the card out loud. (For some of the kids, the words *down* and *sit* were tough words to read.) When they gave Boo the verbal command and he complied, they would praise him out loud and give him a treat for doing it correctly. The kids enjoyed giving the treat, and Boo enjoyed getting it, so the exercise was a win–win for everyone.

Although some kids needed help from Penny with the reading, each child except for Matthew came up in turn and read a card out loud. All were happy to have Boo to themselves for this "trick," and some, like Heather, gave Boo a big hug and a kiss after he got his treat. Eventually, it was Marc's turn. He was a delicately built boy

314

with café-au-lait skin, brown eyes and a sweet smile. He approached with an impish grin, clearly delighted at the prospect of Boo doing a trick for him.

I thought about what Penny had told me about Marc. He had never said anything—not at home and not at school. When April, his mom, said, "Good morning," he'd just stare at her. Meals were a guessing game. She could only hold up different foods and wait for him to point to his choices. When she asked him what he wanted to do on a day off, he simply looked at her without speaking and shrugged. The day Marc came home from kindergarten with scratches on his back, April and her husband couldn't get any clue from him about how they'd gotten there. It wasn't until she called the school that she found out another student had been bullying him during recess and bit him.

At six years old, Marc had never spoken a single word to anyone. Marc's parents tried speech and behavior therapy, and when that failed, they enrolled him in Penny's class for kids with special educational needs. Penny was working diligently with her staff to help Marc begin to feel at ease enough to speak in class. Although they hoped a dog would bring wondrous things to all the students, they knew better than to expect much from Marc, especially because he spent time with many of his relatives' dogs without any effect on his selective mutism.

The card Penny held up said *sit*. Marc stood in front of it, his mouth closed. "Do you want to say anything to Boo?" Penny asked. Marc didn't answer.

"Go on, Marc," said one of the fifth-grade helpers. No response.

"I know Boo will sit if you ask him to," I said.

Marc, the boy who had never spoken a single word in his life, opened his mouth, and an almost inaudible sound came out of it. I heard a soft whispered, "Sit," more air than voice.

I was a bit disappointed as I gave Boo the hand signal to sit. I didn't understand the disorder well and had hoped for more, but an almost inaudible whispered word was better than nothing. So I said, "Excellent. Great job, Marc! Do you want to tell Boo anything?"

Marc leaned over to Boo's ear. He mouthed the words, "Good boy," gave Boo his treat and a big hug and danced back to his place in the circle.

Boo and I left our first visit with the Stepping Stones crew encouraged, thinking it had gone well. I knew Boo's butterfly wings would get him where he needed to be. I knew he would get there, but I just didn't know how far he would take himself.

Sometimes, I think Boo probably has an even more dramatic effect on people than I realize.

Often, I can see progress during a visit, but unless someone reports about ongoing progress, even when there are repeat visits, I never know his full impact. In this case, though, I found out. Penny told me later that the whisper from Marc was just the beginning for him. That night when Marc's mom, April, got home from work, she noticed that he was practically bursting with excitement. Sensing something was up, she asked, "Did something happen at school?"

Marc, the boy who had never spoken a single word to his mother, his father or any other family member or friend, looked at his mother and in a full voice said, "Boo."

"Boo who?" she asked.

Words began spilling out of Marc's mouth, his voice growing louder and louder. "I petted Boo! I brushed him! I love him!" The little boy raced into his bedroom, grabbed his Scooby Doo toy and began to act out the entire therapy session, using the stuffed dog as a prop. This time, it was Mom who was speechless as she listened and listened and listened to her son for the first time in his life. Then, he said four words she'd begun to assume she would never hear from her son: "I love you, Mommy."

"It was as if a door had opened," April told Penny later, through tears, "and we could finally see what was inside. Thank goodness for Boo. That dog is a miracle worker."

• • •

That old pattern-creating universe arranged things so that the day after Boo's first visit to Stepping Stones, my reproductive specialist called to let me know we needed to start injections the next day.

Just after midnight on the day the injections were to begin, Lawrence, who was sleeping downstairs because of a bad cold that he didn't want to pass on to me at such a critical time in the fertility process, crawled his way upstairs to tell me he couldn't breathe. I took one look at him and knew he needed help—fast. It was clear that he was in a horribly bad way. Within seconds, we were in the car, and I was driving like a madwoman. I made the thirty-minute trip to the hospital in just under seventeen. With a blood-oxygen level in the seventies (normal is between ninety-five and one hundred), he needed oxygen immediately, but that was the last information I got on his condition for three days. Lawrence hadn't gotten the forms to sign that would allow the doctors to talk to me about his condition, and Lawrence himself couldn't tell me much because he was so doped up.

With no idea how good or bad things were, and figuring Lawrence would be home soon, the reproductive specialist and I decided to go ahead and start the IUI meds. Waiting would only make my eggs older and less cooperative.

Furthermore, if they were giving Lawrence steroids, which my doctor figured they were, the sperm he produced in a couple weeks would be subpar, so now was really the best time given all the information we had.

By Tuesday, I finally got administration to bring him the right HIPAA forms so the doctors would talk to me, and by that afternoon, I understood that he was in very bad shape. No matter what they did, they couldn't get his blood oxygen above eighty-four, and they wouldn't let him leave the hospital until it was at least ninety-four. I was in a meteor shower of stressors in the middle of this IUI cycle, worrying that Lawrence was in deep medical trouble. He was on oxygen, being injected with steroids and other medications I couldn't even pronounce, and there was talk of a lung biopsy. Meanwhile, I was shooting up daily with the Follistim, trying to figure out how we were going to pay for both the expensive meds I was on *and* the ongoing hospital stay. (The doctors refused to release him, and the insurance company refused to pay for another weekend in the hospital. Every woman in the middle of infertility treatments gets the lecture from her specialist: relaxation and low levels of stress are essential for better fertility. However, if stress truly is a contraceptive, I wonder how any woman anywhere ever gets pregnant.)

Our specialist called me on Friday to let me

know that the egg—the one and only egg I could produce—would be ready to pop the next morning. At the time, I was teaching three classes on Saturday mornings, and the thought of making forty-eight-plus calls to let people know I had to cancel class—not to mention the question of what I would say when they asked why—would leave me with an unbearable response. The plan was to get up at 3:30 a.m. to feed and walk the dogs, zoom to the hospital to pick up the sperm deposit by 5:45 a.m., then get on the road to the reproductive specialists no later than 6:00 a.m. This was either going to be the biggest bust or the funniest story we would ever tell our children.

"Where did I come from?" they would ask.

"Well," we would say, "when two people love each other very much, they drive through the middle of the night to the hospital to pick up the sperm to transport it to a doctor who will put it in the right place to find the egg that will become a baby."

I don't know how I managed to get through the day, but I did—dogs, sperm, reproductive specialist, classes and all. Nevertheless, two weeks later, on the winter solstice, the blood test came back negative.

Since Dad's death, the holidays had grown darker and darker, but this Christmas was my lowest point yet. Lawrence and I spent the day alone at home, making a roast and watching old movies. I called Mom to wish her a Merry Christmas, but when I tried to reach out to my sister and her family by calling them on Christmas, they were annoyed that I had called during dinner and never called back. I hadn't told anyone other than Mom about our assisted reproductive quest. I hesitated in telling her, knowing that the whole family would treat it as nothing but fodder for derision, but because things had improved between us and she was so down after Dad's death, I took a chance that she would be supportive, and it might cheer her up. I realized that when Mom was gone, too, I would officially have no family left but Lawrence and the dogs. She was happy and supportive, and I swore her to secrecy.

The only positive aspect of that Christmas was that Lawrence was home from the hospital and finally terrified enough to start taking care of himself. He was even inspired by the twelve days in the hospital to begin running and exercising.

All we could do was hope that Lawrence and I could create a family based on the love we had built and learned over the years rather than the dysfunction our families had taught us. We only had enough of the very expensive FSH for one more round, and we geared up to begin the IUI procedure again, hoping that the steroids

Lawrence was on in the hospital would be out of his system and that the stress levels of the last round would not repeat themselves.

The only activities that were helping to lower my stress levels, even just a little bit, were my visits with Boo to Stepping Stones. If Lawrence and I couldn't have a child of our own, then at least we could join Boo in helping those who were already here.

When Boo and I arrived at our next Stepping Stones visit, Penny told me the wonderful news about Marc and his response to Boo. As she finished telling me the story, she started to cry, so of course I started to cry because who could respond any other way? That was only the beginning, she continued. Days after Boo's first visit, when she heard an unfamiliar voice tell one of the students, "Get in line!" she was riddled with goose bumps as she turned around to see it was Marc talking in line like all the other students. There were now days, she told me, that she actually had to tell him to use his indoor voice in class. It was a breakthrough that no one could have predicted, and no one could explain. Although there are still times when Marc lapses back into silence, he's made incredible progress. As his mom April said, "Now that he can finally tell us how he feels, we're discovering his personality. He's still a very sweet, loving boy, but now he's a talking sweetheart—with a lot to say!"

We know that dogs and other animals lower our stress and anxiety levels and that there is an anxiety component to selective mutism, but why now, and why Boo? Was it just timing? Was it something that Boo exudes? Was Boo a mirror for these kids, like he was for me, because of his learning disabilities? Could the kids feel him understanding them? These are the mysteries of AAT and the human–animal bond. Marc began to sleep each night with a photo of Boo under his pillow, cuddling with it like a security blanket. Even after my silly, clumsy and often daft dog went home, his presence continued to bring Marc the courage to keep on talking.

I well up with tears every time I think of that month. It was an incredible gift to learn that Boo gave a lost little boy back to his parents by shattering the silence that kept Marc imprisoned in lonely isolation. At the same time, Lawrence and I were devastated that we hadn't conceived a little boy or girl of our own. The levels of irony were almost epic, although we were briefly encouraged, hoping that if a miracle happened for one child and his family, maybe there would be another miracle for us with our second IUI. The Follistim only helped me produce one egg the last go-round, so the doctor took me up to the maximum dosage of 900 IUIs. Yet, after three days on that nuclear dosage, there was zero sign of any egg lurking in my ovaries.

My body was shutting down. We had exhausted our supply of $5,000 FSHs, and there was no money for more. Lawrence had been out of work without pay for three weeks, our insurance didn't cover infertility treatments or a good chunk of Lawrence's hospital stay and now Porthos was having troubles again.

Dante and Porthos had always been the best of buddies. Matched almost identically in size and play style, they would body-slam each other with big, huge, happy grins, rapid-fire play bows (where their front ends go down and back ends stay up, as if they were engaged in some kind of medieval jousting contest that required courtly bows) and other play indicators. They routinely played tug with anything from a large toy to, eventually, the tiny remnants of that toy. When there were no toys around, they often simply mouth wrestled while we all lounged on the bed getting ready for sleep.

There aren't many species on this planet that play into adulthood: humans, dogs, cats and a few others. Researchers are still working out all the reasons for play. Because it requires much energy and can be injurious, it often doesn't fit into standard models of the furtherance and preservation of the species. Play for dogs builds community, allowing them to work out communication skills, and from an evolutionary point of view, it allows animals to role-play, if you will, the skills they would need for survival: wrestling, tugging, digging and even reproduction. The trick is that many of these games require immense trust because one dog's mouth might be right up next to or in the other dog's mouth. Dante and Porthos always had this level of trust with each other.

That is, until one cold, snow-covered day when Dante tried to play with Porthos in the backyard, and everything went horribly wrong. Whirling around, Porthos went straight for Dante's throat, and all Dante could do was try to defend himself from the younger aggressor. At his age, Dante came in at about the equivalent of a seventy-five-year-old human. He was horribly outmatched by the spryer Porthos, whose four years of dog life made him around thirty-five in human years. Shaking with fear, I finally separated them, probably screaming the whole time, while Boo paced in a circle around us, worried and howling. The snow was covered with blood. Porthos had a few scrapes, but Dante seemed badly wounded. I put Porthos into the crate—thank goodness he had a reliable kennel-up command—and took Dante immediately to the vet's.

Porthos hadn't even signaled. He'd exploded from play to aggression. It was unusual for a dog's personality to change like this: an adult dog's established normal behavior will remain that dog's behavior, with slow changes that come with age and experience (unless, of course, we are shaping behavior through training). So, whenever there is a sudden change in behavior, we have to ask if the dog's overall health has changed. Big, dramatic changes like this are usually an indicator of health or neurological changes.

We managed Porthos carefully around Dante and Boo. I watched for any indication that his inflammatory bowel disease was flaring up, but he seemed fine. A week later, wanting to let the boys all have a good time together in open space, Lawrence took the three of them for a walk in the woods. Not more than three minutes after they left, he came running through the back door, Dante at his side.

"Porthos is dying!" he yelled. "Come *now*." Dante's expression was a mirror of Lawrence's: a combination of worry and terror. I threw down my sewing and ran to join them.

Boo, meanwhile, never left Porthos's side. When we got to the spot in the woods where Porthos had gone down, Boo was standing there, watching out for his charge and howling his usual coyote-like howl—whether warning or pleading for help, I will never know. Normally, when Boo is left to his own devices in the woods, he simply wanders from one scent to the next, like he had years ago on the walk with Cindy and Julie when we first diagnosed his disabilities. But this time, Boo remained in place, watching Porthos, perhaps in disbelief or perhaps to protect the dog he once cared for as a baby dog.

This kind of protective behavior isn't uncommon for dogs. They have been known to protect one another from threats or outsiders. In the wake of a devastating earthquake and tsunami that ravaged Japan in 2011, rescue workers came upon two dogs, one injured and the other guarding him, refusing to let anyone near his injured friend. The workers were eventually able to persuade the vigilant guardian to let them approach, and the two dogs were rescued. I have to assume that Boo was protecting Porthos in this way, refusing to move from his post.

As Lawrence and I approached, we could see that Porthos was frothing massively at the mouth, whirling in circles without any control, stumbling over himself, his back end tucked so much that his tail appeared to be lost under his body. He barked wildly and menacingly at nothing that I could see, and even when I called his name and stood in front of him to get his attention, it was as if he didn't recognize me. I had no idea what could be going on.

Eventually, I got my hand through Porthos's

collar and brought him back to the house. He continued to bark wildly and stumbled over himself the whole way back. Boo stayed at his side every step.

When Porthos was secured in his crate, Lawrence described the events. It sounded as if Porthos had a massive, knockdown seizure. I thought back to the altercation a week before. Sometimes small seizures in dogs can present themselves initially as sudden bouts of aggression. Panicked, I called Julie and Cindy at home on a Sunday. Julie, bless her, was home and told me to give him some Xanax, which we already had for the anxiety associated with his inflammatory bowel disease, and watch for any further neurological signs. If any appeared, I was to take him to the emergency clinic.

There were no more neurological events, and after watching him closely for the next week, the final pieces came together when Porthos went into diabetic ketoacidosis. He was hospitalized for three days. I brought him home each night to keep his anxiety under control, sat up with him most of each night to make sure he didn't seize again and then took him back to the hospital first thing in the morning for treatment.

Porthos's ability to go under things never fully developed after the trauma he'd gone through with the grooming table, and given the level of anxiety it would create for him to be in the cages at the hospital, the staff agreed to tether him to the cages in the procedure room, even though nose to tail he made a five-foot-plus obstacle around which the staff had to work. I will be forever grateful to them for this. At one point during his hospital stay, one of the doctors was worried about his level of energy and asked Julie and Cindy whether his behavior was normal, just lying there doing nothing. That question reminded me of the third graders who called Dante lazy. "No," came the answer, "he's just got a really great settle."

The only thing that seemed to be going right for us around this time were Boo's visits, in particular his visits to the Stepping Stones classroom. Boo loved visiting the sisters at Maryknoll and hearing the stories the kids would read to him at the library, but he was the mascot for the kids at Austin Road and seemed to know how important he was there. Marc continued to blossom, reading aloud more, drawing more, participating more. He drew picture after picture of Boo surrounded with red, glittering hearts. Penny predicted that Marc would eventually catch up with other kids his age and that he should expect to have the life every parent hopes their child will have.

By now, Boo's effect on Marc had become a source of inspiration and community for the rest of the kids in the Stepping Stones class. For weeks after the first time Marc spoke, the other kids cheered every time he opened his mouth. "Thanks for talking to us, Marc!" they would say, or, "Marc, you talk great. Good job!" As he was lavished with praise, the shy little boy blossomed, but that wasn't the only thing that was going on. Positive-reinforcement trainers know that when we praise our dogs for doing well, it makes us feel good, too (simply put, positive thinking can release serotonin, the happy neurotransmitter), which means that the simple act of all the kids working together to support Marc helped all of them. Boo's miraculous work with Marc didn't only include the humans. After seeing how he responded to Boo, Marc's family got him a little rescued Jack Russell, adding another save to Boo's record.

Visit after visit, more members of the class experienced their own Boo miracle. Alexander, for example, was sweet and attentive, patiently waiting for his turn to be with Boo, always following directions very well. I was shocked when Penny told me that Alexander suffered from severe ADHD and that before Boo started coming to class, he regularly erupted in frequent tantrums, couldn't hold a still position for more than five minutes and never made eye contact with the other kids. This was not the Alexander that Boo and I knew. There were no tantrums, he stayed seated for the entire hour of our visit and even after the dog left, Penny said, Alexander remained calmer and more focused for the rest of the day. "The dog has brought out Alexander's caring side," she continued, "and he's blossomed both socially and academically. It's amazing that an animal has such a healing power." Alexander improved so much that he was able to start attending mainstream classes twice a week. His parents were so impressed with their son's progress that they made plans to get him a rescue dog of his own. By my count, this puts two *more* saves in Boo's win column.

Boo's career and our infertility treatments continued along parallel paths. We were thrilled to find that Boo was nominated as a finalist for the Pet Partners' national Beyond Limits Award for an outstanding AAT team, and we got the news just as we were moving into the world of donor eggs. Once again, I was hopeful that this was a sign of good things to come. Lawrence got a better job with good health coverage, so we would get at least *part* of one round of the very expensive infertility treatment covered, and Mom insisted on helping out, too. Boo was on *CBS Evening News*, in our local papers and even in the *New York Post*, and animal fans nationwide were voting for their favorite Beyond Limits finalists in a YouTube election. At the same time, we had our first batch of fertilized donor eggs implanted. I couldn't be more thrilled for Boo: win or lose, the little dog who everyone thought was a dullard was chosen from thousands of entries to be a Beyond Limits Award finalist. Even Dante hadn't made it that far.

The first implantation of fertilized donor eggs didn't take, and although Boo didn't win the most votes, my overall joy at his successes kept my spirits up despite the infertility battle. After the second batch of implanted donor eggs, we were overjoyed when the doctor called to tell me that I was "a little bit pregnant." It seemed that all our hopes had been well placed. He said the hCG (human chorionic gonadotropin, the hormone that indicates pregnancy and is measured in home pregnancy tests) numbers weren't great—they would have produced a negative on a home pregnancy test—but they were high enough to indicate pregnancy, and he was guardedly optimistic. The pregnancy was heavily supported with progesterone shots, and for a few weeks, Lawrence and I watched the numbers creep up little by little. I recognized the physical state I was in from times before when I'd thought my period was just very late. This was a particularly painful revelation for me: it meant that at least a few times I had actually been pregnant naturally but lost the baby.

At six-and-a-half weeks into the pregnancy,

there was some bleeding, and the doctors said the hCG numbers were dropping. I had miscarried. They stopped all support and told me to keep coming back into the office to make sure the miscarriage went appropriately, or I would need a D&C procedure. It seemed that my body was telling me no, it was not going to support a pregnancy. My heart was shattered, and Lawrence withdrew into himself.

We never had a direct conversation about how we felt. Our feelings were all over the floor in a heap, and the only approach we could take was to try to slog through and organize them. We had spent his entire bonus that year and then some, as well as the money gifted by my mother to pay for the treatments. I had no strength emotionally or physically to go back to blood draws, injections, diets and the blame that comes from the loss. I was wracked with self-inflicted guilt: *Did I work too much? Did I eat the wrong thing?* Even if we had any faith left in our ability to get pregnant, we were too broke—emotionally and financially—to keep trying donor eggs. It was clear to both of us that repeated rounds would just be deflating and depressing.

It was time to begin the domestic adoption process. My age disqualified us from almost every possible means of adoption save for Friends in Adoption, and even they knew it was going to be almost impossible for a birth mother to choose me over the hundreds of better mommy options out there. By the end of the three-year average waiting period, I would be older than many young grandmothers. Still, it was all Lawrence and I had to hope for.

He was sure that we would be chosen quickly. "Why wouldn't a birth mother or birth parents choose us? We have a lot to offer."

"That's besides the point," I would say, trying to hide the echoes of my family in my head that told me that regardless of what we had to offer a child—a loving home with loving parents, creativity, sensitivity and wonderful animals—no family would want me. I just had to hang onto Lawrence's hope and focus my attention back to the faces eager to see Boo and whatever silly games I had ready for them.

One little girl named Heather liked giving Boo kisses and hugs, but she also loved the care-taking exercises, such as brushing Boo or—her favorite—the Boo-Boo Boo game, which made everybody laugh, kids and adults alike. I would buy a box of silly kids' bandages with Scooby Doo or Sponge Bob on them, and the kids would take turns fixing a pretend boo-boo on Boo, just as their parents fixed their boo-boos. For many of them, the simple act of taking a bandage out of the wrapper, pulling the tabs off and placing it somewhere on Boo—and focusing enough to do it—was a big effort, but the prospect of seeing Boo covered with silly bandages by the end of the exercise was a great incentive. The kids would tell Boo to feel better as they dressed his imaginary wounds. Remarkably tolerant Boo delighted at the attention and naturally just didn't care that there were countless bandages clinging to his furry body. (Fear not, no Boos were harmed in the making of this game. I made sure to remove all bandages with the utmost care, without pulling out hairs.)

Another game the kids squealed over, and the one I most enjoyed putting together, was Where in the World Is Boo? I would ask Lawrence to make silly photoshopped pictures of Boo in various places on the planet and sometimes in outer space, too. I told the kids that Boo was a great explorer and challenged them to guess where he traveled to by the surroundings in the picture. Once they guessed the location, I would show them pictures of various things Boo might pick up on his travels, and the kids would have to identify them. When I held up the silly black-and-white picture of Boo wearing a pith helmet, floating in bad perspective next to the pyramids, Alexander alone shouted, "Egypt!" The kids clamored to gather around the images of the treasures Boo collected on his adventure and correctly identified games, vases and other artifacts from the ancient civilization. Penny was impressed at their focus and level of abstract thinking in these games, but I wasn't surprised that Boo could make even geography fun. Lawrence put a silly Jacques Cousteau hat on Boo for his trip to Paris to see the Eiffel Tower, and once we even managed to land him on the moon.

In return, each time Boo came to visit, the kids showed him pictures they'd drawn of him, Boo holiday cards and a crown they'd made for him. They even wrote a story about him that they illustrated with their drawings. Even when he wasn't present in the classroom, Boo was still motivating this group of very special kids. For Matthew, the boy who'd stayed as far away from Boo as possible during the first visit, the regularity of Boo's visits—and the class's focus on and love of Boo between visits—was a gift. It wasn't just Boo or other living dogs that terrified him; Matthew even refused to play with stuffed animals. Yet, each visit, he was able to move much closer to the circle.

When we desensitize dogs to a trigger, like I did with Boo to my truck when he was still a puppy, we can't rely on language and abstract processing to explain that the trigger won't hurt them. With people, however, just discussing something that is scary in joyful terms—the way the class talked about Boo when he wasn't there—can help the desensitization process.

When Matthew participated in drawing pictures of Boo, making Boo cards and telling Boo stories, he was using abstract processing and forming a positive association with Boo. Every time Boo came to Stepping Stones, Matthew looked more interested and excited. By the third month, he was in the circle with the other kids. Boo couldn't quite approach Matthew for a hello yet, but he could walk close by, especially when Matthew was enthralled by some of our sillier games.

One day we were playing Red Rover, Red Rover, Let Boo Come Over, in which the kids line up in two lines across from each other and call Boo back and forth between the two lines. One child would help me walk Boo across the gap and then exchange places with the next child in line. During this game, the unimaginable happened: Matthew allowed Boo to glide past him so closely that the dog's fur just brushed his skin. Matthew didn't even notice at the time, but when everyone congratulated him on his courage, I could tell how proud he was of himself. Soon afterward, he would even hold the end of Boo's leash (with me holding the leash in between) to walk around the circle for Duck, Duck, Boo. The black Lab mix had finally gained the boy's trust, and Matthew was never separate from the Boo festivities again.

The fact that Penny was able to fill me in on the

children's progress between visits was an incredible gift to me. It's invaluable for me to know what's working during visits so I can tailor the activities appropriately, either continuing with a successful activity or changing it to make it more effective. It's also the purest form of positive reinforcement. Hearing stories like Marc's, Alexander's and Matthew's tells me that the time away from my husband and dogs at home, or away from clients and classes, is very well spent. Whenever I slouch at the inconvenience of getting Boo ready for visits—the weekly nail grinding, the regular teeth brushing, the baths, the inspections right before each visit—all I have to do is remind myself how much of an effect he has on the people he visits, and I straighten right back up again. I think about all the lives Boo and Dante have touched and remember why I got into animal-assisted visiting in the first place: to share the healing powers of dogs and to show just how strong their love can be. There is no greater gift we can give to ourselves than to give happiness to others.

My journey with Boo, a journey that began on that magical Halloween day, has been one of humility, gratitude and joy. He taught me that all of us learn at different speeds and that although not all dogs may be able to learn the same things or perform the same tricks, we all have our hidden strengths and abilities. He taught me that there was no reason to choose harsh punishments and training methods when gentle methods work better and build a better relationship. He taught me to disregard the silly notion that a dog who doesn't comply with a command is being dominant. I think back to that long year of potty-training Boo and how he shut down in class with the über-puppies. Thanks to Boo's patience with me, instead of assuming a dog is being stubborn or dominant, I ask myself, *What is that dog telling me? Is the command unclear? Is it that he physically can't do the behavior? Is he afraid?* It's not my job to dominate a dog; it's my job to understand him, and with that understanding, I will get what I need from the dog. When I do my job properly, it makes me a better trainer and probably a better human being.

Boo taught me to have faith in a dog to learn, even if the pace is slower than expected. I shudder to think what would have happened to Boo in another home. Dogs who don't house-train quickly don't usually get to stay, and even if they do, if they also have trouble learning simple commands—like to sit and lay down—they're often ignored and left to languish. In the wrong environment, dogs with Boo's initial level of fear and anxiety are typically crippled by that fear and run a huge risk of becoming fear-biters, often ending up in shelters or being euthanized.

But Boo didn't just teach me about dogs, he also taught me about life. He taught me to be patient with others, to understand that we all work within our own limitations and more important, he taught me to be patient with myself. He taught me that *different* doesn't automatically mean *bad* and that the parts of myself I've always seen as disabilities might actually, in some circumstances, be advantages. To this day, I'm not sure if Boo was such a successful therapy dog despite his disabilities or because of them. Dante may have been funnier and more entertaining, and Porthos may have been smarter, but Boo—with his love of people, his clumsy snuzzles and his funny gait—taught me that sometimes disabilities and differences can be the greatest, most powerful assets.

Boo taught others, too. He taught Lawrence that he could be a good father and gave him the faith and courage to want a family of his own. Boo brought warm snuggles at night curled up between us. Although he was not the dog I originally wanted him to be, never becoming a service dog for Chuck, Boo proved he was better than I could have dreamed—having gifts for more than just one person—and I suspect Chuck would have approved of Boo's other career plans. Boo wasn't able to help Chuck when he lost his power of speech, but Boo was destined to give Marc the gift of speech. Without the early (if ambitious) training I did with Boo, he would never have become a Pet Partner. The road that led Boo to help Marc and so many others began with bitter disappointment, but it ultimately led to a truly spectacular series of gifts—gifts that for some, like Marc, only Boo could have given.

Boo turned out to be so much more than I could ever have imagined. He's not bright. He doesn't do tricks. He bumps into things and usually has a confused look about him. I often work with clients who are disappointed and frustrated by their dogs' behavior. I remind everyone that the universe doesn't always give us the dogs we want; it gives us the dogs that we need—and the dogs that need us. It's up to us to discover their gifts and forge a loving partnership to help us all realize their true potentials. By doing so, we can learn and grow in ways that may surprise us. Ultimately, that's the true magic of the human–animal bond—and the true miracle of Boo.

Epilogue

Boo is now in semiretirement, visiting only a couple times a month during the fall and winter. His eyesight is almost completely gone, but with a little extra guidance from me, he can still enjoy his visits to see the sisters at Maryknoll and read with the children at the Mahopac library. The Stepping Stones classroom was cut from the special education program at Austin Road for financial reasons, and Penny has moved on to the middle school. Although Boo no longer gets to see his buddies from that truly spectacular class, we will both always have those kids in our hearts, and I'm guessing they will always have a bit of Boo in theirs.

Our family was finally made complete by our adopted son. Boo now snuzzles with a child of his own while Lawrence and I recollect Boo's lessons as we parent our child.

In August of 2010, Dante let us know that it was his time to leave us. He was being eaten alive by cancer and had a few strokes. Julie came to the house, and we were able to let him go with dignity on the pillow he loved to lie on, basking in the sunny warmth of the yard he loved to play in. When he was gone, we brought

Porthos and Boo out to say goodbye. Boo, just like he did when Porthos was having his seizure, would not leave Dante's side as Lawrence wrapped Dante and prepared him for his trip to the crematorium. It's hard to know what Porthos was thinking when he bolted out of the house with his usual zeal, stole one of Julie's sandals, lay down next to Dante's lifeless body and proceeded to roll on his back fervently. In the past, actions like this would always have gotten Dante up with a bark and a chase game to police the pesky Porthos. I can speculate that like a child confronted with death for the first time, Porthos was trying to desperately wake his big brother up from the big sleep that none of us quite understand.

Boo, however, seemed to recognize death from Atticus and, being the good little soldier he is, stayed with Dante all the way to the car, as if on some level he recognized that this would be the last time he would be with Dante. A few friends of mine, Jill, Linda and Teddi, had all come to be with us. Dante was surrounded by visitors and loved ones on a warm, sunny, early fall day. Although we were having the worst day we could imagine, he had the best day we could give him.

That evening, we grilled veggies for dinner in an attempt to make things feel a little bit normal. I always throw the vegetable butts into the woods for the critters; we don't need compost, and the critters like the goodies. Headed out the living room door to the veggie spot over the rock wall, I was thinking of Dante when I looked up. No farther than six feet from me was a big black bear just standing next to the deck looking at me.

"Well, hello there," I said. We both paused for a moment, looking at each other before the bear casually trotted off, looking back at me occasionally as he went. The markings on Dante's back had always reminded me of brown bears because his markings looked like the pattern of lighter fur across the bears' shoulders. In the twelve years that we've lived on this hill, we've never had a visit from any of the black bears who live in our area, and I suspect we never will again. I knew in that moment that this was a sign: Dante was happily trotting off to wherever it is that our dogs go when they die, and he was telling me that somehow it was okay, and he'd be back.

In the days that followed, Boo bumped into things more and more frequently. We realized that Dante had been guiding him, either intentionally or simply by his mere presence, as if Boo had learned to follow Dante's sounds to navigate through the house and yard. Boo was sad again after the loss of Dante but not as lost as he was after Atticus died. Perhaps we all get used to loss in our lives. Porthos was a bit quieter and moped a bit more than usual.

Just six weeks after Dante left us, a pregnant dog came up from a shelter in the South to the Animal Rescue Foundation in Beacon, where I'm the trainer and behavioral consultant. The mamma dog, Ginny, was soulful and sweet, with dramatic eyeliner that made me instantly think of Dante's expressive eyes. Diane Pennington used to say they reminded her of Cleopatra. The rumors were that the father of Ginny's puppies was a stray beagle. Lawrence and I wondered if Dante had taken us literally when we asked him to come back to us as something smaller next time, say, in the beagle range. That was Dante: always fast to respond and always literal. When Ginny gave birth, we started the bio-sensor work with the puppies on day three. They were some of the sweetest, snuggliest, most soulful puppies I have ever seen in the shelter, and Lawrence and I fell in love with a little girl who had the same bear-like saddle as Dante.

It's good to get puppies out of shelters for their physical and mental health, so I fostered them for a couple weekends just before they were ready for adoption. Both Boo and Porthos took to the little girly girl we picked, and we made it official: we had our first girl dog. On New Year's Eve, the one boy dog was not doing so well, so I took him to see Jack, a nearby vet and friend.

None of the other puppies were sick, and the little boy responded well to treatment. The little guy was better in three days, but then the girls started getting sick. They went downhill fast, and ultimately parvovirus was diagnosed. The boy, Pinball—named for his ability to bounce back from illness, his personality and his energy level—stayed with us while all the girls went into intensive care for two weeks. When we finally brought the girly girl Callie (also known as Callily-Baby-Girl's Bagel) home, we thought she was out of the woods, and knowing the difficulties inherent in keeping siblings from the same litter, the impish little Pinball went back to ARF to find a forever home.

Ten days later, our sweet, snuggly little girl had a massive seizure. She died at the shelter's vet's office an hour later. The pain of losing Dante and then Callie so quickly after that was just too much, and I was ready to go from Three Dogs Training to "Two Dogs Training" for a while. However, driving home from the vet's after Callie's death, broken by so many losses in so little time, Lawrence said, "We can't leave the little guy all alone at the shelter."

All his siblings were adopted, as was his mom, Ginny. The snuggly little boy, who spent all of his life to that point sleeping on top of or up against one of his littermates, was all alone in a small, single-dog cage at the shelter. A gentle soul who loves everybody, Pinball is a barker when he's in his element, and a speed demon who darts around at the end of his leash like a yo-yo. I knew from the beginning that Pinball would be hard to place because he was such an energetic, beagle-barking nudge. It was a good bet that he'd be bouncing back to the shelter from one home to another. The next night, he became our fifth little boy dog. He nudges Boo regularly and has been bullied twice by Porthos. Pinball is learning to read his brothers, and now it is clear from his level of energy, his intelligence, his joie de vivre and his desperate attachment to me that he has a good bit of Dante in him. Once again, I was reminded that the universe gives us the dogs we need or the dogs who need us—not the ones we think we pick. I wonder if I will ever have a girl dog.

Boo continues to do his best to take on the caregiver role of this youngster even if he bumps into things and falls over rocks while trying to protect the little ball of energy when Porthos pounces a little too hard. Boo will insist to his last breath on taking care of his charges, and I know he will be at both Porthos's and Pinball's sides to the end.

It is Pinball's turn now to teach me something new about dogs, training and people. He is the first dog I have ever had who loves doing tricks. By four months, he had already learned the trick,

Would you like to apologize? As soon as I ask this question, he lies down and puts his head on his two front paws with a sorry, soulful look up at me, which always makes me laugh. As he works to become Boo's replacement on the visiting circuit, I hope Pinball will rise to the challenge of walking in Boo's paw prints. With his super-social ways and his love of tricks, he has great potential, but only time will reveal his true calling.

Once again, I marvel at the gifts each dog brings us just when we need them. A time will come when Boo and Porthos will have to move on. I know that through that sadness, there will be Pinball at my feet, lying upside down, his front paws crossed over each other in the most impish of poses while he gives me the silliest of doggie grins and wriggles around until I laugh. It is easy to see that the universe sent us this pinball of a dog for the times ahead.

Atticus, Dante, Porthos, Pinball and most especially Boo all know what I have to be reminded of every day: "God grant me the serenity to accept the things I cannot change, courage to change the things I can and wisdom to know the difference." And in my case, a dog to guide me to that wisdom.

Acknowledgments

There is no getting around the fact that without Boo or any of the dogs who have been my companions—Atticus, Dante, Porthos, Callie and even the crazy Pinball—this book would not have been possible. There are so many things I am grateful for from these dogs but space and page count limit me to a simple statement of gratefulness to "The Boys."

For all the humans who played a role in the shaggy dog story that was necessary to write the Boo book, I am grateful to:

Penny, who called the media for one story; Lisa Cool, who saw the big story; Joy Tutela, who never lost faith and whose gentle encouragement made this book as much as words did; Joel Derfner, whose patience and writing talent kept this book from becoming an epic tome to rival *War and Peace*; Sarah Pelz, whose Zen-like editorial level-headedness kept the project moving along; Brooke Jacobs, who made sure Boo looked perfect for his cover shot (and did well by me, too!); Lawrence, who walks beside me along this sometimes bumpy path; and all the dear friends and colleagues who offered support, strength and encouragement: Jill, Linda, Teddi, Bonnie, Kim, Julie, Laura-Ann, Michele and Adrianna, too.

Center Point Large Print
600 Brooks Road / PO Box 1
Thorndike ME 04986-0001 USA

(207) 568-3717

US & Canada:
1 800 929-9108
www.centerpointlargeprint.com